PRAISE F̶̶̶O̶R̶ ̶S̶O̶U̶L̶B̶L̶A̶Z̶I̶N̶G̶

"The Imposter Syndrome affects many people, even highly successful people. Lisa does a brilliant job of breaking your Imposters down and understanding where they came from—which helps you soar in every aspect of your life."
—Kimberly Meredith, medical intuitive and author of *Awakening to the Fifth Dimension: Discovering the Soul's Path to Healing*

"*SoulBlazing* is a powerful method for guiding you through your own emotional wilderness. Lisa's principles are a master key to unlocking self-awareness and living up to your exciting true potential in life. An engaging, lively book filled with pure wisdom. I loved it!"
—Dr. Joe Vitale, star of the documentary *The Secret* and author of *Zero Limits* and *The Miracle*

"I've known Lisa for a hundred years. Her stories and the way she connects with her readers on the stage are mesmerizing. She is a true storyteller and game changer. Her SoulBlazing model has helped many people, including me. I'm honored to know her and to have shared the stage with her."
—Ben Vereen, Tony Award–winning Broadway legend, actor, dancer, and motivational speaker

"This insightful book, SoulBlazing, brilliantly written by the talented Lisa Haisha, is a wonderful guide for serious seekers of self-truth on their journey to the soul. Through profound archetypes that Lisa identifies, we are confronted with our own complexes through the deceptive archetypal masks that we inadvertently hide behind. Lisa's book identifies seven dark shadow archetypes that reside within each one of us: the Victim, the Egotist, the Seductor, the Fixer, the Judge, the Joker and the Overthinker. Lisa skillfully introduces these psychological Imposters and offers helpful solutions to heal. She uncovers our potential for an epiphanous awakening. Our ultimate purpose is to vanquish the internal bête noire and reinstate ourselves in the rightful realm of grace, light, and consciousness."

—Sue Wong, fashion designer, creative intuitive

"This is a most important book to be read now because it provides the psychological and spiritual guidance our society desperately needs at this time. *SoulBlazing* exudes warmth, compassion, and perspicacity and is the work of Lisa, who is dedicated to the well-being of humanity."

—Faith Harrington-Boutin, managing editor of *FVM Global Magazine*

"A remarkable source of insight and the missing piece in my own journey. There are so few teachers to advise us on issues involving both awareness and the soul. Lisa offers guidance on restoring our wisdom of the soul. This is the holy grail of understanding and living a more soulful existence. Written in a style that reflects profound intelligence, sincerity, and real beauty, this book has nudged me back onto a viable path."

—Bobby Joyner, singer-songwriter and reformed lawyer

"I hope you will join me in reading Lisa's new book. Lisa's travels have put her in contact with Sufis, shamans, and spiritual leaders, uniquely qualifying her to help navigate life's issues. She imparts her wisdom through her masterful storytelling skills and makes it highly relatable. There is no one who both understands the soul's journey like Lisa does and can explain things in such a concise, understandable manner."

—Larry Namer, cocreator of the E! Networks

"Lisa has created a deep awareness in me in order to align my intellect, mind, and body with the whispers of my soul. She has taught me that I can manifest a meaningful life by letting go of the conditioning that held me captive. My inner journey in earnest begins now."

—Anoop Kumar, hotel-chain owner and bestselling author

"Lisa got my attention when I first heard her speak. She is a masterful coach and change agent who has been helping people in every walk of life and around the world through her SoulBlazing method. This is cool stuff. What she teaches really works. This book sums it all up. She reads into your soul. A must read."

—Roy Smoothe, No. 1 bestselling producer, presenter, and publisher of music and motivation programs

"This book is a profound source of finding inner peace, which is our ultimate goal in this life. When we start living at the level of soul instead of body or mind, we enter a beautiful world of serenity, love, freedom, and joy. This book offers a beautiful soul journey toward enjoying the real essence of life."

—Dr. Gurmeet S. Narang, bestselling author of *My Happiness* and founder of a spiritual-retreat center in Mumbai

"Lisa Haisha has a special gift and a huge heart, and it comes through in her new book, *SoulBlazing*! Lisa shares the insights and strategies that will help you have major breakthroughs in your life. I've witnessed it happen as she has shared one-on-one with me and my Inner Circle as well as speaking to large audiences. I can't recommend Lisa and her new book enough!"

—Kyle Wilson, host of *Success Habits of Super Achievers* podcast, founder of Jim Rohn International and kylewilson.com

"Lisa's book will get you to listen to the heart of your soul, your true self, your passion, and your purpose for being. She will have you looking in a mirror you never knew existed, a mirror that shows your true beauty. She helps you live the life you should be living. Lisa blesses you with the gifts that show you how to give yourself a rebirth so you can make a change to live your best life! Lisa believes in you. Now it's time to believe in yourself."

—Kathy Buckley, motivational speaker,
comedian, actress, and advocate

"This book is a gift. In her engaging style, Lisa articulates her unique perspective on the mysteries of the human personality with her entertaining, pesky, but well-meaning cast of Imposters, who reside somewhere between our Authentic Soul and our experience of the world. The Imposters step in to help us survive childhood and can endow us with "superpowers," but too often they steal the show, holding us back from a realization of our true selves. Recognizing who they are and what part they play in our day-to-day lives is the first step to freedom. The book may be gloved in velvet, but it packs a spiritual wallop. Like the *Mathenas* of her youth, Lisa is not afraid to provoke, confront, and "blaze" your soul into a recognition of its true nature. Her section on tools and exercises is invaluable and provides an actionable way to blast through unconscious behavior patterns and ignite personal transformation. Lisa's generosity, wisdom, and badassery shine through in equal measure, and she invites you to match her fearless spirit with your own. Study this book, do the work, and watch 'shift' happen."

—Kathryn Douglas, producer and director
of HGTV's *House Hunters*

"Lisa Haisha is the No. 1 SoulBlazer in America—in fact, she's the No. 1 SoulBlazer in the world. I can say that with authority because Lisa is the woman who invented SoulBlazing—a groundbreaking avenue to personal growth and leading a more purposeful life. Now, for the first time, the tools and insights are available in book form. If you're on a self-improvement journey, you will absolutely want this invaluable guide."

—Lee Aronsohn, cocreator of *Two and a Half Men*
and executive producer of *The Big Bang Theory*

"I love Lisa's stories. They are unique and layered due to all her life experiences from traveling to over sixty countries. Lisa has worked with individuals and led retreats and workshops on six continents while creating her life-changing Imposter Model, which is a gift to artists and everyone who wants to discover who they are at their core and how to accept and work with the dark shadows that Lisa calls Imposters. This book is a game changer."

—Maria Conchita Alonso, award-winning
actress, singer, and former beauty queen

"Lisa is a nurturer and a beacon of strength and kindness. Her yearning to help people in ways that improve their lives is magnificent. I hope you cherish her book, as I do. Lisa writes with her heart and her intellect in perfect synchronicity. I'm honored to know her as my forever heart sister."

—Claudia Wells, actress and businesswoman

"*SoulBlazing* is a clear and concise distillation of Jungian archetypes (the Imposters). Lisa Haisha elegantly blends science and her personal experience. This is the perfect book for recalibrating your compass and is especially helpful if you lost yours."

—Frank Ferrante, author and subject of the award-
winning documentary *May I Be Frank*

SOULBLAZING

SOULBLAZING

Transform Your Imposters into
Superpowers and Live a More
Purposeful, Authentic Life

LISA HAISHA

RISA
PUBLICATIONS

Published by Risa Publications

Edited and designed by Girl Friday Productions
www.girlfridayproductions.com

Cover design by Paul Barrett based on a design by Daniel Will-Harris
Icons designed by Daniel Will-Harris
Project management: Kristin Duran and Laura Dailey

ISBN (paperback): 978-0-578-31785-4
ISBN (ebook): 978-0-578-31965-0

This book is dedicated to all the beautiful souls on their journey of self-actualization, becoming emotionally free, and finding inner peace.

The most important kind of freedom is to be what you really are. You trade in your reality for a role. You trade in your sense for an act. You give up your ability to feel and in exchange, put on a mask. There can't be any large-scale revolution until there's a personal revolution, on an individual level. It's got to happen inside first.

—Jim Morrison, interview with *Cinetropic*

CONTENTS

INTRODUCTION

*The soul has been given its own
ears to hear things that the
mind does not understand.*

—Rumi

Everything has an origin story, including this book. I've spent decades traveling around the world, and these experiences informed the SoulBlazing insights that I'll share with you. But the real roots of my work go back to my childhood, because like you—and like everyone on this planet—most of my formative experiences took place during my early years.

I grew up with an Iraqi father and a southern belle American mother. I have four sisters, one of whom is my twin. We felt lucky to have each other as we navigated our childhoods. We were a tribe of girls with dueling cultures, growing up under a Baghdad roof in sunny Southern California. What would possibly go wrong?

Naturally, both of my parents brought their own cultural history into the family. My father's cultural distributions were loaded down by the strict patriarchal Middle Eastern values that informed *him* while growing up. Girls were supposed to be nice, quiet, obedient, and subservient to their (preferably Iraqi) husbands. Anybody who strayed from the status quo was suspect in his mind, and everything we did should conform to social conventions. How did that play out in life?

Here's an at-a-glance list of my father's parenting rules that I walked away with, which were verbalized or implied:

- *Never trust strangers. Don't even smile at strangers. (But if you must smile, don't show your gums. It's unladylike.)*
- *Don't travel unescorted, show your midriff, smoke, or drink.*
- *Don't tease or perm your hair, or cut it above your shoulders.*
- *Keep your legs crossed when you sit, and extend your little finger when you drink tea.*
- *Never kiss on a first date.*
- *Never kiss on a second date.*
- *Never talk back to your husband or question him.*
- *Never gain weight or be too thin.*
- *Have sex only to have children, but don't enjoy it.*
- *Don't talk too much.*

The list went on and on. Now that I'm a parent, I have perspective and understand that my father was not only trying to protect us but also seeing the world through his own lens: He'd lived through war, revolution, civil unrest, and poverty in Iraq. Now here he was raising five young girls all close in age in Southern California in the wild 1970s. By the time we were teenagers, the freedoms we enjoyed were all risks in his eyes—as some of them should have been, considering what was going on and that he had five teenagers at the same time.

At the time, however, I took all his rules at face value and felt oppressed by them, as most teenagers do by rules. But I also admired his work ethic, his leadership skills, and how liked he was by everyone. My mother was a different story. (I'll get to her later in these pages.)

I feel that for the first part of my life, I was pretty tame. After college, I wanted to live more fully, even if I got scraped up a bit, because I felt so restricted as a child. I had a strong urge to challenge myself and explore life more deeply. I wanted to push limits through traveling around the world mostly alone and see where I landed. I wanted to feel what it would be like to not care what other people thought, which is tough when you're born into Middle Eastern culture. In Iraqi culture, we're taught to care about other people's judgments before we make any choices. I was on a quest to figure out who I was without the constraints of pleasing others and getting their approval first. I sublimated my own freedom and desires in order to satisfy the invisible judgments of family members against hypothetical wrongdoings. That behavior was oppressive and made it difficult for me to self-actualize: Who was I truly, authentically, deep down?

But certain aspects of my father's culture actually opened my eyes rather than closed them. I vividly recall going to Chaldean Iraqi funerals, where women called *Mathenas* were hired to help people grieve the loss of loved ones. (This is common in many cultures throughout the world, notably in Japan.) In my childhood memory, the Mathena was a sort of badass grieving coach who'd call out people in harsh ways to provoke their grief.

I sublimated my own freedom and desires in order to satisfy the invisible judgments of family members against hypothetical wrongdoings. That behavior was oppressive and made it difficult for me to self-actualize: Who was I truly, authentically, deep down?

She might wail to a mother: "You could have sacrificed more for your son. Now that he's gone, you're crying? You could have done more."

Or she'd lament to another relative of the deceased: "Your close friend died. He was family. You could have helped him more. When he needed a loan for his business, you didn't give it to him. Now he's gone, and his depression probably killed him."

After the loss of a parent, she'd rail at the kids: "You mourn your mother now, but where were you when she was in the hospital for several months? You were too frustrated with your mother's demands, so you stopped coming by to help her. You were not a good child."

I was always astonished watching this. It seemed like theater, but the Mathena's goal was to deepen the truth of a situation and provoke people to open up and release their pain—even if whatever she said wasn't entirely true.

Years later I checked my memory with my relatives, who told me that the Mathena wasn't nearly as harsh as I recalled. But provocation *was* part of the process. She'd push them to feel vulnerable, sad, even angry. The goal was to help them grieve, forgive (themselves and others), and ultimately release unresolved emotions so they could get on with life and grow. It was about stripping away the masks. In many ways that part of my childhood became the genesis of SoulBlazing.

I SPENT MY EARLY ADULT years working as an actress, which scared my protective father crazy, but it had been my dream since I was ten years old. He called daily to make sure I was safe and came to LA every few months to check in on me and my roommate, Eve Selis, who was (and still is) a fabulous singer and close friend. He wanted to move us out of our "roach-infested apartment," but we loved it and refused to move because we wanted our authentic success story. In his worldview, actresses were whores. I thought he was over-the-top with that statement, but after a few months of auditioning and working in Hollywood, I understood his reasoning. Actresses weren't whores but rather prey for some of the successful men who were in control. After I met a couple of them, I quit. The business side was too much for a Chaldean girl, even though I thought I had shed a lot of the "old me" and felt more liberated. I guess my overprotective father's message did get into my head more than I thought it did. I couldn't even imagine doing a love scene or nudity, especially knowing my dad and other family members would be watching me.

Hollywood was a training ground for learning about not only the masks we wear in actual theater but also about the emotional masks people wear to protect themselves or project a false image to the world. I also learned about my *own* masks and how my ego hid various fears. For the short while I was a rising star in Hollywood, I lived the fast life and tried to be someone I was not. I was unable to play that game for long. I flamed out and left the acting world when my agent called with a modeling job in Japan. Thrilled to be leaving Hollywood, I packed my bags and headed to Tokyo, where I became the unlikely face of the city on billboards. Imagine Bill Murray's character in the film *Lost in Translation*, and you get the picture.

Japan was an intensive cultural immersion boot camp for me. I soaked up the nuances of this Asian milieu and loved how radically it veered from my own American world—particularly when it came to geishas, who've been an integral part of Japanese culture since the eighteenth century.

I was fascinated by geishas. They are literally trained to entertain and be subservient to men. They not only wear actual masks, but they're also the ultimate Seductor Imposters (but we'll get to that in pages to come). The first time I saw a geisha in Kyoto moving down the street like a swan, I was determined to meet her. She wore a kimono wrapped tightly around her impossibly tiny body, with jet-black hair perfectly bound in a chignon. I followed her to a Japanese hostess club called the Lion's Den in the entertainment district of Gion. Her face was layered with thick makeup, but her eyes reflected a vague sadness.

I managed to lie my way into the club, fooling the doorman into thinking I was a "new girl" who'd come to work there. The place looked like a 1970s discotheque, complete with colorful mirrored balls and flashing lights. It was packed with drunken Japanese businessmen and hostesses who seduced them with theatrical come-ons. The whole place was like a masquerade party, with fake names for the men, fake identities for the women, and fake smiles and laughs all around.

As my eyes darted around the room, I got it: The seduction fantasy was real enough to mask the emotional pain that people experienced in their daily lives outside the club. These women were instant therapy to the men, "instant love," wearing their own literal masks. This kind of charade still thrives in Japan, where companies actually "lease" people for holidays and special engagements. You can rent a spouse, a couple of kids, cousins, grandparents, nieces, and nephews. It is a profoundly beautiful culture based, in many ways, on masks and Imposter identities.

After my experience in Japan, I'd gig-work, save my money, and take off to soul-seek in other countries. More of a listener than a talker, I'd often get lost in people's stories—a listening skill that became a serious part of my coaching practice. So many of my SoulBlazing insights were gleaned from encounters with wildly different people around the world: I danced and broke bread with members of the Maasai people in Tanzania who taught me how a simplified, uncluttered life soothes the soul and who showed me the profound importance of community. I interviewed prostitutes in Amsterdam who affirmed that difficult choices need not keep you from forgiving yourself and moving forward. Working with orphans in Iraq (whom I later memorialized in my book *Whispers from Children's Hearts*), I learned how a harsh reality can be lived with either a positive or negative attitude—and how the latter can derail your life.

These travels only deepened my thirst for understanding human nature. Back in the States, I got my degree in spiritual psychology and revisited the theater world, studying improv at the famous Groundlings Theatre and the equally renowned Lee Strasberg Theatre & Film Institute in Los Angeles. I loved improv: it was group-focused, and believe it or not, it tied in perfectly with my psychology studies. Improv gives people a safe space to play and to embody different personas and scenarios, which is at the root of visualization and manifesting one's reality.

When I'd talk people through issues that they needed to heal or resolve, I'd often get more clarity and creative solutions if we both wore different hats like in improv: We'd become different personalities, in essence, and act out certain scenarios. Other aspects of their own personalities would ultimately emerge in telling ways as they dropped their guard and allowed their subconscious to take center stage. Sometimes things emerged that were linked to deep-seated emotional issues—things that the more analytical mind would otherwise repress.

After calling those personalities several different names such as "the voice in your head," "your dark passengers," and "your relatives," the name "Imposters" came to me. Suddenly, it all started to come together.

I went into private practice, but I still felt like something was missing. When I got the opportunity to work with inmates at the Chowchilla prison outside Fresno, California, I was thrilled. Within weeks, I was working in a hard-core women's state prison in the middle of nowhere. Here I met Bella, an inmate who had no interest in a "traditional" style of coaching.

Bella made *Breaking Bad* look like *Breaking Good*. She had a shaved head and tattoos that wrapped around her bulging biceps like snakes. She was in for life after committing murder—twice. And she was impenetrable. She'd had a tragic, nightmarish childhood and dared me to even *think* about showing her any compassion or concern. Her default position—which was clearly a way to protect her wounded heart—was to be rude, verbally aggressive, and a bully.

I decided to veer off course and venture into new coaching territory, which involved taking cues from my acting background. I didn't realize it at the time, but I was also channeling my inner Mathena.

"Who do you think you are, you arrogant bitch?" she sneered when we first met. "I've seen therapists and coaches and fucking counselors for twenty years, and not one of them has been able to help me. Your degree means shit to me. How could you ever understand or relate to what I've been through?" Then she looked me up and down and added, "I hate your fucking briefcase."

Initially I was shocked and thrown off-balance. Actually, I hated my briefcase too. I'd grabbed it on my way out the door that morning to give myself more of an authoritative air. But it was bullshit—and Bella knew it.

Somehow her calling bullshit on me gave me the determination to do that same thing to *her*. Deviating from the standard script given to volunteers, I decided to "mirror" Bella: I'd let my own Egotist Imposter off the leash (though at the time I didn't have a term for it), confront her like a Mathena, and shock her out of her own bullshit.

I inched my chair closer to hers and got in her face, leveling my gaze. "You know what your problem is?" I asked in a steely voice.

She froze.

"You're mean," I continued. "You're filled with darkness. You have no empathy or heart. In fact, you have the devil inside of you. You've hurt a lot of people because you act like a victim. You act like everyone owes you something for the pain you've suffered."

That was all it took. "You fucking can't say that to me!" she yelled. "Who the fuck do you think you are?" She looked like she was about to jump me and throw me across the room. I held up my hand.

"Wait," I said. "I *can* say that to you because I also have the devil inside of *me*. I have darkness inside of me as well. It's part of human nature."

She looked back at me, confused. I pressed on. "Bella. We all have darkness in our hearts. We're humans. This is our school: Earth is our school. It's not easy to be human. I may not have murdered anyone, but I've certainly hurt people, psychologically or emotionally. But today you have a choice. Right now. Today. You can make shift happen."

"How can I make shit happen when I'm in jail?"

I smiled. "I said 'shift,' not 'shit.' You can make *shift* happen in your life. You ready for that?"

She cracked a smile back. In that moment Bella began to soften. "You have the choice, Bella," I went on. "You can forgive your past and those who hurt you, and choose to start a new story as the heroine who escaped hell and is now a healer and wise woman. You can change your life in an instant. I dare you."

No one had ever mirrored Bella's mask back to her. No one had ever pushed her like a Mathena. But now Bella was starting to let down her guard; she was vulnerable, not volatile. I could feel her Authentic Soul in her gaze. So I did something that threw her even more: I pulled up my chair, held her hands, and gazed into her eyes for a few seconds. I sent her love, and then I told her that I loved her. She immediately broke down in tears.

Bella was releasing her pain—and there was a lot of pain there. Finally, with tears streaking down her face, she said, "Lisa, you just blazed my soul."

In that moment, SoulBlazing was officially born. SoulBlazing is a practice for blazing through your emotional baggage so that you can live a more purposeful life that's aligned with your

Authentic Self and your Authentic Soul. The radiant clarity that comes with this type of personal development and transformational work is super vital. I call it a soul practice.

The book you're reading now is the culmination of many years and countless hours of SoulBlazing work helping people get in touch with their Imposters. In my work I've identified seven of them that you'll explore in these pages. There are, no doubt, other Imposters, but I have seen these seven Imposters regularly in my work with clients.

This book will help you identify and release the emotional obstacles and masks that impede your personal growth. The ultimate goal here is to align your personality with your Authentic Self in a deep, soulful fashion, and ultimately to live with a sense of clear purpose. While each Imposter has negative aspects that impede you from living from your Authentic Soul, each also has its positive qualities. I call them superpowers. Ultimately the goal isn't to banish the Imposters from your life, but rather to learn how to leverage the positive aspects of your dominant Imposters and use them to help you navigate any situation or relationship with ease. When that occurs, you'll be able to SoulBlaze your life.

READY OR NOT, THE TIME TO DO SO IS NOW.

PART ONE

SUPERPOWERS OR SABOTEURS?

The VICTIM

The EGOTIST

The SEDUCTOR

The JOKER

The FIXER

The OVER THINKER

The JUDGE

CHAPTER 1

What's an Imposter?

*You either walk into your
story and own your truth, or
you live outside of your story,
hustling for your worthiness.*

—Brené Brown, *Rising Strong*

I'm sure you're all familiar with the two masks that represent the theater. They actually have names: Thalia is the laughing face of comedy, and Melpomene is the sorrowful face of tragedy. Their origins go back to the golden age of ancient Greek drama to show the two extremes of the human psyche. But the Greeks should have come up with more than just two masks. In reality, we put on many masks to express different aspects of our psyches or, frequently, to *hide* them. I call these masks our Imposters.

Before we dive into our Imposters, let's recall the awesome power of masks: Since time immemorial, we humans have worn elaborate masks for all sorts of religious ceremonies and cultural rituals. Masks are worn to honor or mourn the dead, heal the sick, enact mythological events, and guide spirits to the realm of their ancestors. They are also worn for fertility rites and can transform the wearer into a god, a hero, or even a demon. They're so awe-inspiring that we collect them and display them in museums.

In Western culture, masks transform us into all sorts of supernatural and imaginary beings during Halloween. At masquerade balls, they hide our identities and our "imperfections" so we're emboldened to flirt with people we wouldn't dare approach in "real" life.

Each mask represents someone or something powerful, in both the positive and negative sense of the word. In the world of SoulBlazing, each mask we wear represents an Imposter. In my work I've identified seven of them that prevail.

OK, so what exactly are Imposters?

Imposters are seven archetypes that we develop to protect ourselves from various insecurities and wounds that we experienced during our childhoods. They are as follows:

1. *The Victim*
2. *The Egotist*
3. *The Seductor*
4. *The Joker*
5. *The Fixer*
6. *The Overthinker*
7. *The Judge*

These Imposters live in our psyches. They're like a series of masks that we wear for so long that we start to identify with the falsehoods they represent. You could also consider them like a cast of characters that lives on the stage of your brain and calls the shots. We hide behind them so well that we sometimes even live double lives: the mask on the outside, that's the face of our Imposter, and our inner world that drives what's really going on deep down. Often there are conflicts and contradictions between the two.

Although Imposters can be our biggest emotional saboteurs in life, they can also be our biggest superpowers, depending on how self-aware we are. And becoming self-aware is a big part of the SoulBlazing process, which goes hand in glove with cultivating your emotional intelligence.

Emotional intelligence, otherwise known as EQ, is the ability to manage your emotions in ways that enhance your communication with others, allow you to handle obstacles, and help you respond productively rather than react rashly. Psychologist Daniel Goleman has identified five key attributes of EQ:

1. *Self-awareness*
2. *Self-regulation*
3. *Motivation*
4. *Empathy*
5. *Social skills*

These five key attributes are a by-product of SoulBlazing work.

Our Imposters feed on the insecurities we developed as children. And one thing is clear: we all internalize wounds and develop strategies to protect ourselves. These strategies feed our Imposters.

If you felt emotionally abandoned as a kid, for example, you probably learned to maintain emotional distance from people in order to protect yourself from the pain of abandonment. (That's called sabotage, by the way.) The result is that you have a hard time sustaining meaningful emotional relationships with people.

Or maybe you were so belittled growing up that you developed an overinflated ego to protect yourself from feelings of self-loathing. On the outside you seem like you have your shit together. Maybe you're even bold and boastful. You've got an Egotist Imposter *and* a Seductor Imposter on overdrive. But inside? Inside you're a scared, insecure little kid crying out for attention. Your overinflated ego became a strategy for hiding that little wounded kid.

Whatever the case may be (and we'll explore a lot of cases in forthcoming chapters), these behaviors eventually became patterns that informed your personality; that remained the case even when, as a grown-up, your circumstances changed and those behaviors didn't protect you at all. On the contrary, they actually *created* obstacles that often undermined your best interests. Nine times out of ten, however, you're unconscious of this. Your Imposters are in the way, lingering in your subconscious.

Understanding your subconscious *and* your conscious mind is the key to cultivating self-awareness. So let's unpack them both.

The conscious mind is the striving, analytical part of our brains where we judge, assess, and try to make sense of the world. It's expressed through our personalities. The subconscious mind

Being responsive is the opposite dynamic: It's like being emotionally anchored in the calm depth of the sea, where the waters are clear and still no matter what's happening on the surface.

is what's going on *underneath*, in the unseen emotional realm where our wounded inner child dwells. Basically, the conscious mind is like the hardware of your computer. The subconscious mind is its operating system. It's composed of code—or all those underlying patterns and connections that were laid down during your childhood. You can't see that code, but it runs the show. It's the engine that determines how you react to the world at large versus how you respond to it.

And the difference between being reactive and being responsive is the difference between night and day.

Every Buddhist philosopher and garden-variety wise soul will tell you about the power of being responsive to the world, rather than being reactive to it. "Whatever happens in your life, joyful or painful, do not be swept away by reactivity," Buddhist nun Pema Chödrön tells us in *When Things Fall Apart* (2016). "Be patient with yourself and don't lose your sense of perspective." Those of you old enough to remember martial artist Bruce Lee might recall him saying a simple version of the same thing: "Be like water."

"Be like water" became a trope long before the internet was born, but Lee's full quote went further: "Empty your mind, be formless," he said. "Shapeless, like water. If you put water into a cup, it becomes the cup. You put water into a bottle and it becomes the bottle. You put it in a teapot, it becomes the teapot. Now, water can flow or it can crash. Be water, my friend."

Being reactive is like experiencing the world on choppy seas, always at the whim of the weather. You're tossed about by your emotions and triggered by your fears, anxieties, and insecurities. And you *react* from that agitated place. It's like having road rage of the soul.

Being responsive is the opposite dynamic: It's like being emotionally anchored in the calm depth of the sea, where the waters are clear and still no matter what's happening on the surface. You literally go with the flow. You are, as Lee put it, being like water. Yoga teacher and author Darren Main uses the metaphor of a waterwheel. It "doesn't attempt to change the course of the river," but "it simply surrenders to the flow and allows the power of the river to be expressed through it. Most see surrender as a form of weakness when in fact, surrender is the source of all true power."

Here's what that looks like in pedestrian terms if we take the metaphor of road rage to its logical extreme: If someone rudely cuts you off with their car, you can react, roll down your window, yell something rude, and flip your middle finger at the driver. Then you can drive on, your body flooded with stress hormones, setting the tone for the day in a debilitating fashion. I think it's obvious why being reactive like that is not optimal.

On the other hand, you can "be like water." You can simply respond by accepting that you were cut off on the road by a driver. That happens. Instead of being reactive, you simply let the car move along and resume your path on that same road. You don't own their rage because it belongs to them; it doesn't belong to you. (More on that concept appears in the "Tools and Exercises" part of this book.)

Of course, that's easier said than done. Often we don't even know why we react to things. But every day we have a choice about whether we react or respond to life. The first step in that direction is becoming self-aware and aligning our conscious and subconscious minds, where our Imposters live. In short, it's about *becoming aware of our Imposters.*

In my work with people from every walk of life, I've identified the seven Imposters that we'll explore in these pages. Before we dive in, let's get this one caveat out of the way: Imposters are not to be confused with Imposter Syndrome. Imposter Syndrome is a psychological dynamic that's expressed in the persistent sense or belief that deep down you're a fraud, even if you're actually highly accomplished. People with Imposter Syndrome invariably dismiss their accomplishments as luck or chance. They are self-deprecating to a fault. They might be running a highly successful multimillion-dollar business and might have achieved every hallmark of success, but deep down they still think that they're a fraud.

This irrational belief is often accompanied by the fear of being *exposed* as a fraud. Sheryl Sandberg, second-in-command at Facebook, told *Forbes* magazine that "there are still days when I wake up feeling like a fraud, not sure I should be where I am."[1]

---

1.   Kerry Hannon, "The No. 1 Way Women Can Succeed More at Work," *Forbes*, April 24, 2014, https://www.forbes.com/sites/nextavenue/2014/04/24/the-no-1-way-women-can-succeed-more-at-work/?sh=7f38efdb17c0.

David Bowie told Q magazine that he was plagued by feeling "inadequate" his entire life. In an interview with Oprah Winfrey, tennis pro Serena Williams spoke about her struggles trying to become her Authentic Self. Tina Fey, Lady Gaga, Natalie Portman—the list of highly accomplished celebrities who struggle with Imposter Syndrome goes on and on.

The jury is out about what exactly creates Imposter Syndrome, though there is consensus that its symptoms are connected to depression, low self-esteem, and anxiety rooted in our early family dynamics.

News flash: there's just no escaping those early family dynamics.

But every day we have a choice about whether we react or respond to life. The first step in that direction is becoming self-aware and aligning our conscious and subconscious minds, where our Imposters live. In short, it's about becoming aware of our Imposters.

It's hard work wrangling our Imposters, but once we identify them, we're on the way to more freedom in just about every arena, from the bedroom to the boardroom. The seven Imposters that you'll discover in the following pages have both positive and negative traits. Chances are you have a dominant one, but all the Imposters exist within us to varying degrees. Personal growth is all about understanding them and unraveling the limiting false beliefs behind them.

We all need to do some amount of emotional and spiritual housekeeping. When we commit to that process, we evolve. We grow. And we get more in touch with our Authentic Souls. That can sometimes be scary. We sometimes so identify with our emotional pain and fears that we don't know who we are without them. Here's a classic example: the chronic dieter who's been trying to lose weight forever but is ultimately attached to being overweight because it's an excuse for not being intimate with people. As countless psychologists will tell you, carrying extra weight can protect us from feeling emotional pain. We end up identifying with being overweight so much that we're afraid of who we might be without it. Realness can be raw and authenticity daunting in its freedom. But in the end, it's way better than the hidden spears of false Imposters. As they say, beware of wolves in sheep's clothing.

Once you start that important spiritual housekeeping work, your Imposters will surely protest. Your Victim Imposter might whine: *I don't wanna do the hard work. Don't make me!* Your Egotist Imposter might lament: *I already know that I can do the hard work, ergo I don't need to do it. I don't have to prove anything to anyone!* Your other Imposters will chime in with their own excuses for not doing the work of personal development. And that's because the Imposters are engrained, are compelling, and present an infinite number of arguments against the case of self-awareness.

But here's the good news: We *can* change. But change is often a process of unlearning things. So many life coaches and change agents preach the gospel of unlearning, but guess what? It's not so easy to do, though the gospel has been around for thousands of years. Greek philosopher Antisthenes is quoted as saying, "The most useful piece of learning for the uses of life is to unlearn what is untrue."

We humans are conditioned at birth to "learn" through our parents and communities to accept biases that inform racism, sexism, religious convictions, political views, and gender identity. It's not until we're older and self-aware that we realize how misguided these biases might be and how much they've penetrated our psyches. We then (some of us) struggle with unlearning these deep-seated biases, but it can be a messy process.

I often equate this with the act of disentangling a messy ball of yarn to understand its individual strands: You take one strand and unravel it from the ball to explore what it is and where it came from. Then another. And another. Until finally you can see how the whole ball of yarn has been spun together into a tight cluster of thought forms and misguided beliefs. This unraveling or unlearning is the first step toward self-awareness, which invariably leads to a deeper connection to your soul.

That's why the case studies in this book revolve around the S.O.U.L. framework: STOP, OBSERVE, UNDERSTAND, LIBERATE. Coupled with an understanding of our Imposters, this practice helps us align our personalities with our Authentic Souls. It shares a common border with the Buddhist practice RAIN. RAIN is an acronym that stands for Recognizing what is happening in the moment, Accepting it, Investigating the emotion around it that comes up in your body, and Nurturing it.

I will use the S.O.U.L. practice in every case study in these chapters to show it in action. The goal of personal development here is a lofty one, I know. And it's also not always easy. But tell me: What worthwhile outcome in life ever is? In my workshops I have the time and space to explore Imposters using improv and other fun games. I've found there is immense power in acting out our personal scenarios so we can view them from different angles and have even more compassion and understanding for all involved.

THE
AUTHENTIC
SOUL

CHAPTER 2

THE AUTHENTIC SOUL

*If you cannot hear the sound
of the genuine in you, you
will all of your life spend your
days on the ends of strings
that somebody else pulls.*

—Howard Thurman, 1980 commencement
address at Spelman College

Our Imposters are showstoppers that occupy center stage in our lives, whether or not we're aware of it. They feed on layers of false beliefs and old stories we tell ourselves about our lives that no longer serve us. These false beliefs and old stories can wreak havoc, preventing us from achieving our highest objectives and being aligned with a sense of purpose. And they influence—often negatively—how we act and what we say. But once we have a practice for taming our Imposters, we're able to get in touch with a much bigger star in the constellation of our lives: the Authentic Soul.

The word *soul* has made its way into every aspect of pop culture, from spiritual retreats to Oprah's Super Soul Sunday. Deep down we all yearn to be soul seekers and SoulBlazers because deep down we *are*, in fact, spiritual beings.

I'm not alone in citing the awesome quote by Wayne W. Dyer. He famously hit that nail on its head when he wrote, "You are not a human being in search of a spiritual experience. You are a spiritual being immersed in a human experience."

How true that is—but how often do we forget or lose connection to this truth? We get *so* immersed in our "human experience," with our Imposters taking up so much precious real estate in our minds, that we lose touch with the fact. We lose touch with our Authentic Souls, never mind our Authentic Selves.

So what's the difference between the two?

Your Authentic Self is connected to your individual purpose and passion in life. It's the real, true, genuine you, at your core. Your Authentic Self is not about your job, your parents, or your religion. It's not defined by the outward trappings of your life. Your Authentic Self is informed by the experiences and hard-won wisdom you've accrued throughout your life. It's also about expression: who you are when you are free and uncensored. Your Authentic Self emerges when you're unburdened by the rash judgments, negative self-talk, fears, and reactivity of your Imposters. Some of us have such a hard time getting there that we self-medicate with drink or drugs (or chronic distractions of any kind) to free ourselves from the torment of our own minds. This is a surefire way to push ourselves deeper into a rut.

Look at it this way: our Imposters are like static on a radio that makes it impossible to tune in to our Authentic Selves. The best way to work through the noise and fiction of our Imposters is to STOP for a moment and get quiet inside, OBSERVE them, UNDERSTAND the fears and anxieties behind their chatter, and LIBERATE ourselves from them. That's right: the S.O.U.L. work throughout these pages is not only a path to self-awareness and your Authentic Self; it's also the path to your Authentic Soul.

The Authentic Soul is a more transcendent part of our human nature. It's not connected to our personalities—or even to our specific cultures, religions, or socioeconomic status in the world. Psychotherapist Carl Jung spilled gallons of ink writing about our psyches, the nature of light and dark archetypes that live in our personalities, and the spiritual longings that reside in our souls. According to Jung, the only way to get in touch with our Authentic Soul is to do emotional and psychological house-keeping. In other words, we have to become conscious.

When "an inner situation is not made conscious," he wrote, "it happens outside, as fate."[2] That's one way of saying that if we don't get our shit together and become self-aware (particularly of our Imposters), we'll keep manifesting the same obstacles and negative patterns over and over in our lives. And we'll never get in touch with our Authentic Souls.

When we're in touch with our Authentic Souls, we also experience that sense of oneness that is the touchstone of spirituality: a powerful, transcendent connection to all things. Some of us find that connection in a church or temple. Others find it on psychedelic journeys or in silent retreats in the middle of the desert.

> **The best way to work through the noise and fiction of our Imposters is to STOP for a moment and get quiet inside, OBSERVE them, UNDERSTAND the fears and anxieties behind their chatter, and LIBERATE ourselves from them.**

But you don't have to go anywhere specific to get in touch with your Authentic Soul. A friend of mine once told me that washing dishes is a meditative practice that helps him get in touch with his spiritual core. And that's because *your Authentic Soul*

---

2. C. G. Jung, *Aion: Researches into the Phenomenology of the Self*, (Princeton University Press, 1979).

is always present. You just have to maintain a practice of self-awareness to experience it.

I spent decades in pursuit of my Authentic Soul in my early years and often tried to wrangle my Imposters. Travel was my drug of choice for escape and connecting to something bigger than myself: between acting jobs I'd pack my bags and head to Europe or the Middle East. I lived and worked in Japan for years as a model, an English teacher, and an actress. I even wrote, acted in, and directed a film in Japan. I had close encounters of the human kind with people from just about every walk of life in over thirty countries around the globe. But the closest I got to being in touch with my Authentic Soul was when I was sleeping under a breathtaking night sky in the middle of the Wadi Rum desert in Jordan. I felt a powerful resonance with a force outside myself—a connection to "God" in that moment, but not in the biblical sense of the word.

In her book *Help, Thanks, Wow*, author Anne Lamott describes God for people who are triggered by the word. She calls it a "force that is beyond our comprehension but that in our pain or supplication or relief we don't need to define or have proof of or any established contact with." And it doesn't really matter what we call that force. Lamott writes, "I know some ironic believers who call God Howard, as in 'Our Father, who art in Heaven, Howard be thy name.'"

Instead of Howard, I call that sense of God the Authentic Soul.

Most of us long to feel the aliveness of our Authentic Souls, but our personalities get in the way. I've read hundreds of books on spirituality and psychology that explore this dynamic. Writers like Hermann Hesse, Albert Camus, Viktor Frankl, Fyodor Dostoevsky, and others were inspirational beacons of knowledge about the human spirit. But it's perhaps spiritual teacher Gary Zukav who, speaking with Oprah Winfrey (and in his book *The Seat of the Soul*, 1990), had the most direct explanation about the soul's relationship to our personalities. He describes the soul as "that part of you that existed before you were born and that will exist after you die. It's the highest, most noble part of yourself that you can reach for." To be whole human beings, he says, our job is to "align our personalities with our souls." And we do that "by becoming the personality that has the same intentions of the soul: harmony, cooperation, sharing, and reverence for life."

Allow me to add, dear readers, that for our personalities to have "the same intentions of the soul," we need to wrestle with the Imposters that take up space in them. Those Imposters have loud voices that drown out our deeper intuition, shouting out self-talk that's linked to fears, anxieties, and false stories we tell ourselves. The Authentic Soul speaks to us in a much quieter voice. It speaks to us when we're alone in nature and through meditation and other meditative activities, including hobbies like knitting or painting. We need to listen to that voice. We need to give it more airtime. The S.O.U.L. practice is the best way to do so.

We can travel all over the world in a soul quest to "find ourselves" and answer proverbial questions about the meaning of life. I certainly did, trekking my way across every continent and ocean seeking knowledge and experience about my Authentic Soul. But as all great sages know, the true path of self-knowledge does not lie on the outside. It lies within.

German philosopher Friedrich Nietzsche once wrote, "He who has a *why* to live for can bear with almost any *how*." Harnessing your Imposters will align you more directly with your Authentic Soul and a sense of purpose, which is all about that "why."

PART TWO

OUR IMPOSTERS

THE VICTIM

CHAPTER 3

THE VICTIM

*You try all your life to be
an adult, but something
deep down inside you will
always be that child.*

—Viv Albertine, *To Throw Away Unopened*, 2018

It's no coincidence that our first Imposter is the Victim. It's the mother ship of all Imposters because it shares a common border with our wounded inner child. And everyone has a wounded inner child at the root of nearly every emotional obstacle in life. I hate to break it to you, but there's no escaping childhood. But there *is* the possibility of transforming adversity into meaningful growth and even personal empowerment. And that's what this book is all about.

Now, I know we've heard the term *inner child* before. We might be twenty years old or a hundred years old, but deep down we all have an inner child who's still licking its wounds. That inner child might also be the source of our creativity and wildest dreams. It might fuel our imagination and be the genesis of our art. It's not all about negative stuff. But it most definitely carries the lion's share of emotional pain that we take with us into adulthood, sometimes with a fierce attachment to the pain despite the burden of its weight.

That's called baggage, my friends. And there's no escaping *that*, either.

What we often don't realize, however, is how our wounded inner child manifests itself in our lives. Because it's a sneaky shape-shifter: our wounded inner child can take on many different personas. We'll get to that shortly.

Before we dive in, let's tip our hat again to Carl Jung, who coined the term *inner child*. In his essay "The Psychology of the Child Archetype," Jung wrote that the inner child "represents the strongest, the most ineluctable urge in every being, namely the urge to realize itself." Which is another way of saying that we all come into this world with a deep desire to self-actualize—an "urge." That longing to become someone unique is at the very root of your being. And that "someone" is linked to your Authentic Self, which is connected to you on a soul level.

If you're triggered by the word *soul*, rest assured that I'm not talking about it in the strictly Christian sense of the word, though like many people I was raised to believe in it. I went to church with my family. I said prayers. I got down on my knees and said "amen" to God, not quite knowing who He/She/It was. But when I got older and traveled around the world, exploring different cultures and religious traditions firsthand in both the East and the West, I realized that religion and spirituality are not the same thing.

I believe that each one of us comes into the world with a soul, which is the unique life energy that infuses and informs our being. That energy, our soul, transcends religion. Some people might call that energy God. Other people call it the Force or the Universe. Buddhists refer to samsara, or death and rebirth (and, by extension, karma).

Our souls are also connected to a specific purpose. Some of us might have a clear sense of our purpose but find it too difficult to manifest. Or we'll spend our lives sabotaging that purpose— that "urge to realize," to quote Jung. In either case, we'll blame other people or circumstances for our inability to fully self-actualize, instead of exploring our own limiting beliefs or self-defeating patterns. That form of chronic blame and "unempowerment" is the hallmark of the Victim Imposter.

Limiting beliefs and self-defeating patterns are rooted in all sorts of childhood experiences. Maybe we experienced actual physical abandonment or abuse. Or maybe the abuse we suffered was more subtle: emotional detachment from our parents, for example. Either way, to protect ourselves we learned on an unconscious level to keep emotional relationships at bay so that we don't have to reexperience the pain of emotional abandonment. To make sure those relationships are kept at bay, we sabotage them without realizing it. Or we blame others for creating

> **I believe that each one of us comes into the world with a soul, which is the unique life energy that infuses and informs our being. That energy, our soul, transcends religion.**

obstacles or not meeting our needs when, in fact, we're not ready to even *face* our own needs. It's like flipping the camera on your smartphone so that it's focused on what's in front of you rather than being turned back at you. The main "issue" is never you; it's always someone or something else outside yourself.

Say hello to your Victim Imposter.

When we were children, chronic blaming and emotional distance might have protected us from pain. In adulthood, they no longer serve us. In fact, they often perpetuate pain. Think of the Victim Imposter as the vulnerable part of you that was neglected, deeply wounded, or never allowed to express itself. This state of mind causes us to mistrust others and harbor feelings of shame and self-doubt, holding on to anger and fear like a trophy. This, in turn, causes loneliness and separation from others, which then makes it even harder to experience acceptance. A vicious cycle perpetuates itself!

What's really going on deep down is a desperate desire for love and approval. But when it's not fulfilled, that desire can hurt. So we have a knee-jerk tendency to blame others or feel slighted over the smallest act. We want intimacy with others. In fact, we might crave it. But since we've never fully experienced bonds of trust, we don't allow intimacy into our lives. (Because remember, it might go away, right?) So we keep it at bay. Maybe we do that by sabotaging a good thing before it sabotages us. Maybe we just live in the comfort zone—prime real estate for the Victim Imposter—deflecting responsibility for self-actualization and blaming others for our own lack of progress. We're too frightened to move into the discomfort zone of life, where personal growth often happens.

I once worked with a client who was so emotionally wounded as a child that his entire adult life was predicated on trying to stay in his comfort zone and be loved by others. Instead of learning to love himself (step one), he offered all sorts of professional favors to people, hustling his personal network to create business opportunities for them. He'd establish complicated quid pro quo relationships with vendors to service others, always with a big unctuous smile on his face, then get hugely resentful when those opportunities weren't reciprocated—even if those opportunities never panned out. Worse, he'd expect compensation even though he himself never invested an actual dime. Then he'd flip a switch and immediately shift into victim mode, blaming others and lashing out like a child. That only distanced people from him, which enraged him further. He set the groundwork for his own failures in this vicious cycle because he didn't do the hard work of looking deep inside himself and understanding the nature of his Imposters.

THE SUPERPOWERS OF THE VICTIM IMPOSTER

The Victim Imposter is not all negative, by the way. People with dominant Victim Imposters are also empathic and feel responsible for other people's pain. They can be endearing, nurturing, and loving. They're good at making people feel important and helping them reach their dreams. That might be you too. But if you're not self-aware, those positive attributes can get the best of you, particularly if you're an empath. There's a fine line between being an empath and owning other people's pain, letting them walk all over you, and not speaking your truth.

When you do the hard work of pushing through your discomfort zones, your Victim Imposter can also be transformative. Invincible triathlete David Goggins is an extreme example of what that looks like.

Goggins had a nightmare childhood marred by abuse, poverty, and PTSD. He grew into a depressed, obese young man with no future prospects. But through incredible self-discipline and dedication, working consistently *way* outside his comfort zone, Goggins transformed himself into a top endurance athlete and elite Navy SEAL, inspiring *Outside* magazine to name him one of the "Fittest (Real) Men in America."

Did Goggins transform himself overnight? Of course not. In his totally transparent book, *Can't Hurt Me*, Goggins chronicles his crazy story of deprivation and despair. "I was very ashamed of my life story," he said on *The Rich Roll Podcast* from January 1, 2019. "I didn't want to go out and tell anyone shit about me. I didn't want people to know that I had all these issues." And that's because despite his current public persona (hard body, super badass), deep down Goggins is a self-proclaimed introvert who had to grapple hard with his wounded inner child—or what he calls his "insecure little kid." But his desire to inspire others was bigger than his shame or his introversion.

Goggins is a testimony to what we humans can achieve when we take our Victim Imposter beast by the horns. He's living proof that, as podcast star Joe Rogan put it, we can all change the course of our lives if we "push harder and dig deeper in everything we do."

That's not just New Age speak, by the way. According to Andrew Huberman, a professor of neurobiology and ophthalmology at Stanford University School of Medicine, neuroscience is teaching us that "the path to courage and success arrives through embracing pain and fear, not by avoiding them." In his pursuit to change his life, "Goggins taught himself how to tap into that elusive holy grail of human existence: the ability to rewire one's own brain in order to continually do better and actually become better, regardless of feelings, external conditions, or motivational state."

Doing stuff "regardless of feelings, external conditions, or motivational state" pretty much defines Goggins's modus operandi. He starts his book with four "Warning Orders." The first one is this: "You are in danger of living a life so comfortable and soft that you will die without ever realizing your true potential." The second one describes the "mission" involved in counteracting this danger: "To unshackle your mind. Ditch the victim's mentality forever. Own all aspects of your life completely. Build an unbreakable foundation."

Of course, Goggins's personal path is not for everyone. But the tools and exercises in these pages are "soft" steps toward the goal of change and personal development. And the principles here, which include embracing your discomfort zone and staying in action, are the same: you need to create an environment for change to happen within, even if that means saying affirmations and hating the process. That might involve showing up in front of the mirror to affirm your self-love when all you feel is self-loathing. Or volunteering your time with the homeless even if homelessness freaks you out. Or meditating in silence even if you can't stand silence and hate sitting still.

What I'm saying here is that things don't happen magically. Artists know that if you wait for inspiration before you pick up a pen or paintbrush, you might sit on your ass your whole life with nothing to show for it. You have to show up and stare at an empty page or a blank canvas every day, come hell or high water, to make shift happen. And you have to stop blaming outside forces for what's not happening in your life. You need to get in touch with the emotional story in your past that no longer serves you.

But here's another little piece of the puzzle: to make *shift* happen, you have to be *ready* to shift. In other words, you have to be ready to let go of your attachment to your former self. And you have to be unrelenting. "I don't stop when I'm tired," Goggins writes in *Can't Hurt Me*. "I stop when I'm done."

THE BEAUTIFULLY DAMAGED VICTIM

As a life coach, I see people with dominant Victim Imposters every day. Paloma is a perfect example: a twentysomething college grad with dark hair and thick black eyeliner, Paloma was a goth if I'd ever seen one. Because she was young, the wounded inner child feeding her Victim Imposter was right on the surface. She was transparent. And quite a handful.

When Paloma wasn't moody and flying off the handle in an irrational rage at the drop of a hat, she clammed up and retreated to her bedroom for hours, if not days. Her grades slipped in high school and her friends were, in her mother's words, "dubious characters" who did drugs and courted trouble. A supremely gifted student who once had aspirations to attend the Juilliard School, Paloma spiraled downhill. She ended up graduating from community college but couldn't find a job. It was "impossible" to find one. She was aimless. Worse, she'd floated the word *suicide* to her mother. Was that a taunt or a threat? Did she really want to harm herself, or was she just crying out for attention? I wanted to get to the root of that.

"Do you want to be here today, or is someone making you come to me?" I asked her point-blank the first time she sat down in my office.

"I'm curious about *you*," she replied with a grin.

I wasn't buying it, so I just looked at her with a poker face. Finally, she sighed and said, "OK, my mother made me come here. She's crazy. She doesn't understand me." She flipped her black hair behind her shoulders and slumped into the sofa. She called herself "beautifully damaged" and clearly didn't want anyone screwing up her sullen perfection or sabotaging her unique creativity. She was attached to the coolness of looking like she'd been ravaged by life. In other words, she was too hip for happiness. Smelled like teen spirit to me.

"Tell me more about yourself," I said. Paloma stared at me and chewed her gum with pent-up anger, smacking her ruby-red lips together. I stared back. We sat there, locked in a gaze. Who would break it first?

Paloma started with small talk. She said that she loved playing guitar and wanted to be a musician. She practiced for several hours a day, but since she never got into Juilliard, she felt like "a big fat loser." She lived on chocolate and cigarettes. She blamed all her woes on other people and circumstances. Her teachers were "fucking stupid." The job hunt was a "waste of time" because employers never got back to her. The music world was "too competitive." And then, of course, there were her parents.

"My parents are fucked up," she said. "My mom is lame. She doesn't have a mind of her own and does whatever my dad says. And my dad is worse. He's a controlling jerk and a misogynist." She rolled her eyes in disdain. "They think I'm fucked up, but they're the ones who have problems. They should be sitting here talking to you, not me."

Having been a teenager myself, I knew the drill: teens often perceive other people, particularly their parents, through a one-sided perspective. Children just don't get how their decisions push their parents' buttons. Being a parent, I see myself as a mama bear with immense love for my daughter and a desire for her to be safe and make good decisions. We parents have decades of life experience that our children don't have, and we want to protect them from pain. When I look back on my childhood, I recall that my parents, even though they were strict at times, were equally loving to my sisters and me. For example: I remember how much my father actually loved us and how hard he worked to put food on the table and put us in private schools. And for a time, my mother would wake my sisters and me with a foot massage (that's five foot massages *every* morning!) and a warm washcloth on our eyes to ease each of us into the day instead of hearing an alarm clock. She grew up in rural Virginia and was raised with a strong work ethic. Her family built their home and had to go to the well for water. My mom had discipline. Even though it was hard on her to raise five girls with no nanny or housekeeper, she still managed to pour out her love and be there day in and day out for the whole family. She was the glue that held us all together, and she rarely complained.

Who knew what the real story was behind Paloma's "lame" mother and "jerk" father? It's only when we become parents *ourselves* that we start to see our own parents as fully dimensional human beings. "What do you want to get out of our time together?" I asked, not taking the bait and throwing the ball back into her court.

"That's your job, isn't it?" Paloma replied, her Victim Imposter in the driver's seat. "To figure out what we do with our time together?" She glanced out the window with feigned disinterest.

Behind her stony mask I could sense something emotional quivering right on the surface—her wounded inner child. I'd coached enough people to know that if Paloma didn't do some emotional housekeeping, she would end up wallowing in victimhood and self-pity, and her twenties would go by in a flash. She'd flounder into adulthood, angry and unfulfilled. And I knew one thing for sure: traditional talk therapy wasn't going to motivate Paloma to open up.

So here's what I did: I moved my chair closer to her and leaned forward. "I'm going to hold your hands," I said. "We're going to look into each other's eyes for a few minutes in silence."

"We're going to stare at each other and you're going to *hold my hands*?" she practically snorted. She looked like I'd just asked her to drink bleach.

"Yep," I replied, reaching out *my* hands. "That's exactly what we're going to do."

EYE-GAZING AND WINDOWS TO THE S.O.U.L.

William Shakespeare is sometimes credited with the oft-quoted phrase "the eyes are the window to the soul," but a thousand years before *that*, Roman statesman Cicero suggested that if the face is the "mirror of the mind," then the eyes are most surely its "index." We human beings have always known that our eyes reveal our true nature. It's nearly impossible to hide emotions in them. "Look me in the eye and tell me the truth," the questioner will say to the accused, because both parties know that while words can mask the truth, our eyes will invariably reveal it.

In his book *The Power of Eye Contact* (2010), author Michael Ellsberg writes that eyes can "speak volumes about a person's emotional state," even if that person is trying to hide it. When we eye-gaze, our Imposters are stripped away because they live on the personality level. Eye-gazing helps us connect on a soul level that transcends the trappings of culture, religion, gender, and socioeconomics. Which way we lean politically, what type of car we drive or job we have, how rich or poor we might be—all of that becomes irrelevant.

And there's even more to it than that: Many of us grow up feeling as if we are not truly seen for who we are; we grow up feeling invisible. The act of eye-gazing galvanizes the simple but extraordinary power of *being seen* in a transcendent but deeply personal way. That's why hundreds of thousands of people poured into a museum to eye-gaze with performance artist Marina Abramovic. Captured in the documentary *The Artist Is Present*, Abramovic sat on a simple wooden chair in the middle of an otherwise-empty room in the Museum of Modern Art in New York. The only other object in the room was another chair, where people sat in front of Abramovic to silently eye-gaze with her. Many of them had transformative experiences and were moved to tears by the intensity of simply being seen. And that's because eye-gazing strips away the artifice of the personality in ways that talking falls short. Being seen in a deep way gives us quick access to real emotions.

But it's not always easy to open yourself up to another human being this way. It can be embarrassing, even overwhelming, so at first Paloma was uncomfortable and fidgety. "Stay still and focused," I told her softly as she squirmed on the sofa.

"Do I really have to do this?" she protested.

"You don't have to do anything," I replied. "But what do you have to lose?" Something shifted in Paloma when I asked her that last question. After around five minutes—it must have felt like a lifetime for Paloma—she fell into it. I could feel the angry Victim Imposter, with its wounded inner child, start to soften up.

THE POWER OF S.O.U.L.

This was the first step in what I call the S.O.U.L. exercise—a practice I employ with nearly all my clients. Here's how it breaks down.

S stands for STOP. We must stop, get quiet inside, calm down the inner chatter, and be in the moment. This is how we can get in touch with the calm center—or the eye of the storm—that exists deep within.

O stands for OBSERVE. Once we STOP, we can observe our emotions with more objectivity and clarity, rather than being swept up in their current. We're poised to be responsive rather than reactive. (Much more on that is in chapters to come.) We can actually "see" our emotions and look at them with more neutrality.

U stands for UNDERSTAND. When we STOP and OBSERVE, we invariably become more self-aware, which helps us understand how our dominant Imposter trips us up. We're also able to understand the roots of our Imposters because we have a certain objectivity; with distance we start to see, in a new light, the challenges during our formative years that created limiting beliefs and negative self-talk.

L stands for LIBERATE. Liberation—release, freedom—is the net result when all three preceding principles are active. When you experience liberation, your entire vibration changes. And when that happens, you actually attract different people and experiences into your life, because like attracts like.

Without the objectivity that comes with the S.O.U.L. process, however, we often stay stuck and attract the very toxic people and experiences that confirm our worldview as seen through the eyes of our dominant Imposter. We stay in the safety zone, where it's easy to blame others for frustrations and get caught up in patterns. And that keeps us in the same life cycle, because we manifest what we believe, even if those beliefs trip us up and create roadblocks to personal growth. As the old adage by Henry Ford goes, "whether you believe you can do a thing or not, you are right." The goal is not to be "right" but to be whole and self-actualized.

THE S.O.U.L. OF THE VICTIM IMPOSTER

Paloma's eye-gazing experience allowed her to STOP. That was step one. After a few minutes of silent eye-gazing, when I felt an inner shift in her, I spoke quietly. "I want to talk to Little Paloma through her Authentic Soul," I said. "And I don't want her to look away. I want her to go to the place where she first felt emotional pain."

I was taking cues from the world of active improvisation that I describe in the first chapter: in improvising the role of her childhood self, Paloma could reply to me as her wounded inner child. She could embody that "Little Paloma" and OBSERVE the roots of her pain—which was step two in our process.

I told her to go back to one of her earliest childhood memories—a memory that might have been difficult or challenging for her. I wanted her to *become* that child while keeping her eyes locked on mine. Paloma nodded. She was ready to take an emotional risk, open up, and be vulnerable.

"Hello, Paloma," I said.

"Hi."

"Tell me where you are and how you're feeling."

She was quiet for a moment. "I'm in Indiana with my mother and stepfather," she finally said. "My stepfather is hitting me and telling me I'm a little shit and that he wishes I didn't exist."

"How does that make you feel?"

"I'm scared. I feel fucking unsafe. I want to kill myself."

"How do you respond to your stepfather?"

"I don't. I just storm off and sit in the basement of our house and think about dying." She was quiet for a moment, then added, "My mom usually just walks away. She's scared of my stepfather and thinks she needs him for her survival. So my stepfather keeps going crazy, then he burns out and clams up. I learned how to protect myself, I guess, by shutting down. Just like him."

"Is there anything you want to say to either one of them?" I asked. "Is there anything you want from them?"

That was all it took: Paloma started to tear up, then she started to sob. What she wanted was attention and acknowledgment from her parents. What she wanted was to feel love, especially from her mom. And she wanted her parents to be happy despite their faults. But somehow, in her vulnerable child mind, she felt responsible for their happiness (and they were both clearly unhappy adults). To deflect this burden, she decided it was easier to try to dismiss her parents and, worse, dismiss herself. She withdrew from the world, then blamed everyone and everything

> **That "no" to her old life was the beginning of "yes" to her Authentic Self. It was a tiny but vital breakthrough.**

for all the things she couldn't do in life. Blame was her consort. Her Victim Imposter was her driver.

Paloma, speaking as "Little Paloma," went on to describe moments of fear and confusion. Using improv as a therapeutic tool, she was able to "become" her younger self and relive distressing moments that she'd internalized as self-loathing. I put "become" in quotation marks because that younger self never left her; that younger self was her wounded inner child—and it was still very much a part of her. But by embodying her wounded inner child as if it were a role she was playing, she was able to actually *observe* it.

"I want to try something with you," I said after doing this inner child work. "I'm going to shift now and play the part of the little girl inside you. I want you to play you in present time."

Paloma nodded. Any resentment or skepticism she had felt when she first arrived in my office was gone.

"I love you, Paloma," I said. "I want you to be happy."

She was silent, but I could feel her suddenly retreat. Something in her slammed shut like a castle drawbridge. "Do you love me? Even a little bit?" I repeated as her wounded inner child, the handmaiden of her Victim Imposter.

"No," she finally replied. "You're a memory of my darkest secrets, a constant reminder that I'm ugly, worthless, and unlovable."

"I don't want to represent that image for you anymore," I said. "I love you and want you to be happy. I want you to have a career that you're passionate about and find a great partner to love. How can I help you reach your goals and dreams? How can I set you free from hanging on to your past? From hanging on to me?"

"You can start by dying," she said. "If you didn't exist, the memories would fade. There would be no memory keeper."

I held Paloma's hands tighter. "If I die, then a part of you dies, too, because we're one. Do you really want to die?"

I gave her a minute to answer the question. We never lost eye contact. She stared into my eyes. Her eyes moistened. "No," she finally replied.

Over the next few sessions, we continued the S.O.U.L. practice. Paloma moved back and forth, from OBSERVING to UNDERSTANDING how her wounded inner child manifested itself as a Victim Imposter that blamed others for her woes. She understood that the "story" of her childhood could be released. She did not have to live it or own it her entire life. It did not have to define her. Slowly but surely, her feelings of self-loathing began to dissipate. Her anger softened and released. She was able to get a grip on her Victim Imposter and open her heart not only to others but also to herself.

Once we go through the S.O.U.L. practice, we start to understand the narratives and false beliefs we have in our heads from our childhoods that no longer serve us. We're then able to see the world through a new framework: We move from Victim to Manifester. We put a leash on our dominant Imposter and let it serve us, instead of being subservient to it.

It's not easy to get in touch with your Victim Imposter or even understand its relationship to your wounded inner child. I know that personally, because I had my own wounded inner child. Growing up with an Iraqi father, I was expected to conform to his rigid social conventions. I had to be a "good girl" in every way: I had to look pretty, be polite, never assert my opinions to others, distrust strangers, and basically stuff any wild, messy desires into a little box.

My American mother felt powerless and like "one of the girls," since she had married at eighteen years old (she met my father when she was fourteen years old) and my dad was a decade older and was the breadwinner. When my mother was eight years old, her mother married an alcoholic, and her life changed. It became chaotic and unpredictable. She eventually found refuge working in a neighborhood beauty salon, where she learned the tricks of the trade. The owner of the salon adored her and taught her everything. That salon was her salvation—and beauty took her away from her sadness and empowered her by uplifting her and teaching her confidence. She loved to see beauty in everything and wanted everyone to feel the magic of transformation through the power of makeup, skin care, and fashion.

When we were in grade school, she wanted us to look as put together as possible. I remember when she lost it when I had messy bangs in my second-grade school photo. Apparently, my mop of hair took away one of the few things she had control over, and she wanted me to take pride in my presentation of myself.

The memory stands out because she rarely lost her temper. She was always the peacekeeper, and many kids on our block adopted her as their mother and therapist because she was empathetic and loving.

These were my parents' stories—stories that were bound up in the insecurities they had while growing up. They weren't *my* story. Still, I tried to own the messaging and be what they wanted me to be. I got good grades and tried to look my best. I smiled at the right people. I was even voted Miss Chaldean, complete with a crown and sash. I was not only nurturing a bit of a Victim Imposter; eventually I also developed a Seductor Imposter to hide whatever was going on underneath all that niceness. I took that Imposter with me years later to Hollywood, where I kept smiling. And looking nice. And posing.

But deep down?

Deep down I was a contemplative introvert with a wander-lust streak who wanted to curl up with a good book. *Alone.* With messy bangs. And read biographies of incredible people who defied social conventions. Short of that? I wanted to ditch everything, get on a plane, and explore far-flung exotic lands and cultures. Traveling was my way of putting on a mask: When I was in a foreign country, nobody knew who I was. I wore the mask of anonymity. That mask gave me the superpower of feeling free. It took me years to become aware of my Imposters and find my Authentic Self without the escape of travel.

You get my drift. We all have our insecurities. Many of us have insecurities that are rooted in emotional experiences far more damaging than what I experienced. My parents were loving people despite their failings; they were far from abusive. Some people aren't so lucky. But for many of us, the "urge" to self-realize that Carl Jung described is often stifled during childhood.

As I grew up, my Victim Imposter expressed itself in a duality: I was fearful of strangers and of taking risks, but I was also wildly curious about the world. I was afraid of other people's judgments, yet I was attracted to people who defied social conventions. And I took a lot of risks. It was only through countless experiences traveling the world, and later through my studies in spiritual psychology, that I was able to see in myself the very archetypes that I now see so clearly in others. I was able to trace the roots of my fears as they expressed themselves in my own Victim Imposter and release them.

Fear manifests itself in curious ways: some people actually fear success, for example. They're so insecure and busy deflecting responsibility and blaming others for their inability to move forward in their lives that they can't even envision the success they crave in life. These "glass half-empty" people blame their bosses, their coworkers, their friends, even the world at large. They constantly compare themselves to other people. As a result, they often have a hard time finding satisfaction in personal relationships. And when those emotional dominoes fall, they really come crashing down.

Your dominant Victim Imposter will keep you in a rut your entire life if you don't tackle it head-on. So you have two choices: You can acknowledge its presence, understand the experiences that formed its roots, and work on becoming aware of the ways you deflect responsibility for your life by blaming the world around you. Or you can keep blaming and feeding your Victim Imposter and live a half-baked life. Your Victim Imposter might feel gratified in that latter scenario (*hey, all my problems were caused by other people!*), but your Authentic Soul will never be fully expressed. You'll give away all your power.

This leads us to our second Imposter, which is all *about* power—a false sense of it. So let's move along to our next chapter and explore yet another saboteur in the pantheon of Imposters.

A QUICK RECAP OF THE VICTIM IMPOSTER

This mother ship of all Imposters shares a common border with our wounded inner child, and *everyone* has a wounded inner child. It's at the root of nearly every emotional obstacle in life.

People with dominant Victim Imposters often harbor deep-seated emotional pain from childhood. To protect themselves from future pain, they tend to deflect responsibility and blame other people or circumstances for whatever is going "wrong" in their life. This mindset only perpetuates self-defeating patterns that prevent you from fully self-actualizing. And that form of "unempowerment" is the hallmark of the Victim Imposter.

But here's the good news: we *all* have the possibility of trans-forming adversity into meaningful growth, even if we've been busy licking our childhood wounds for decades!

The Superpower: *Empathic, sensitive, loving*
The Saboteur: *Stuck in comfort zones, blaming, has difficulty taking responsibility for things in life*

THE
EGOTIST

CHAPTER 4

THE EGOTIST

When two egotists meet,
it's an I for an I.

—Source unknown

Comedian George Carlin once quipped, "One nice thing about egotists: they don't talk about other people." He's right. They don't talk about other people because they're usually too busy talking about themselves. They're full of bombast, which is a front: they might act like they're Masters of the Universe, but in reality they're more like the Wizard of Oz behind the curtain with his pulleys and levers, filled with insecurities.

You'll find this Imposter archetype in every walk of life, but it's rampant among celebrities in Hollywood, the Egotist Imposter epicenter of the universe. Celebrities are a great reminder of what this Imposter looks like at its most extreme and out of control. Swap out "narcissism" for "egotism," and you get the picture in Dr. Drew Pinsky and Dr. S. Mark Young's book *The Mirror Effect: How Celebrity Narcissism Is Seducing America* (2008). Pinsky and Young write that the personal lives of celebrities and their egotistical behavior "have become the defining story lines of our entertainment culture, played out in real time and held up for our amusement, scrutiny, and judgment." This bad behavior, driven by out-of-control Egotist Imposters, is characterized by "excessive partying, promiscuity, divalike tantrums, eating disorders, spectacular meltdowns, and drug and alcohol abuse, behaviors that have become more open, more dramatic, and more troubling than in previous generations."

Does that sound like fun?

When I worked among celebrities as an actress myself, I took that kind of bad behavior for granted. This was way before the #MeToo movement, when men could power-trip and stoke their egos in ways that are unthinkable today.

Fast-forward to current times, when my work in Los Angeles still puts me in daily contact with more Egotist Imposters than you can stuff into a fun house. Let's unpack this Imposter.

THE DIFFERENCE BETWEEN AN EGOTIST AND A NARCISSIST

For starters, not all people with dominant Egotist Imposters end up in a glitzy celebrity rehab center, detoxing on wheatgrass. But many people with dominant Egotist Imposters *do* tend to push the envelope on social protocols, often without even realizing that they're doing so or caring about the implications.

Psychoanalyst Sigmund Freud was the first person to put the concept of the ego on the map over a century ago, back when your great-grandparents were teenagers. (He also had a lot to say about sex, but I digress.) In a nutshell, Freud identified three components, or "agents," of the human psyche: the id, the ego, and the superego. The ego is the more organized, consciously aware part of our psyche that helps us make sense of reality (as opposed to our irrational and instinctual id and the moral high ground of the superego). It informs our sense of self, which is why it's often linked to self-esteem, for better or for worse.

Paradoxically, deep down, people with dominant Egotist Imposters often have *compromised* self-esteem, even though they seem to brim with self-centeredness and what masquerades as self-love. When our egos are wounded during childhood (or when our sense of self and self-acceptance is challenged), we develop defense mechanisms and emotional patterns that emerge as a dominant Egotist Imposter within.

What exactly does that mean? Well, people with dominant Egotist Imposters are generally self-centered and care almost exclusively about themselves. We all know people like this: They're often super charismatic to the point of being bombastic, with a tendency to be aggressive or have a short fuse. They can be possessive and jealous, are offended by criticism, and hang on to past glories—yet they can also be super charming. They love to be on center stage, win every competition or debate, and get in the last word. Their favorite place, in short, is on a pedestal.

A narcissist is an egotist on steroids. In fact, narcissism is a clinical condition that has a place in the *Diagnostic and Statistical Manual of Mental Disorders*, the bible for psychiatric health-care workers. Narcissists are so pathologically entrenched in their own psychoses that many psychiatrists and psychoanalysts shy away from treating them. We find narcissists in the dictators and sociopaths of our world. These people often have visions of grandeur and lack any form of empathy, unless it's for their self-serving entourage. They're the corrupt bullies and tyrants of our world. Many of them were emotionally abused as children, so they grew into emotional abusers and users themselves. And every country has seen its share of them, even the good old United States of America.

People with dominant Egotist Imposters aren't as extreme as narcissists, but they're often confused with narcissists because they share similar traits. Like celebrities, they have an uncommon ability to attract people. In this regard they share a common border with the Seductor Imposter (see the next chapter), only they don't necessarily rely on sex appeal to woo people.

In the workplace, these strong individuals easily lose their temper and rule with an iron fist, keeping everyone on their toes through fear. They like to do things *their* way and generally don't care how that might affect their coworkers. It's their way or the highway—and that highway invariably leads back to them. In other words, it's a huge drag working with colleagues who have dominant Egotist Imposters. As Harold S. Geneen put it, "The worst disease which can afflict executives in their work is not, as popularly supposed, alcoholism; it's egotism."

So how does the Egotist Imposter develop? Well, you might notice a pattern here: all our Imposters are rooted in childhood experiences that often stem from neglect of some sort. Sometimes it's benign neglect—the latchkey kid whose parents were loving but always gone, for example. But when that neglect becomes abusive, things change. The more love is withheld, the more an Egotist Imposter emerges as a salve and protection against emotional pain or loss.

In other words, behind the self-centered Egotist Imposter, there's often a fearful child hiding deep insecurities. The bigger the ego, the deeper the insecurities go. People with dominant Egotist Imposters often didn't feel safe growing up, so they developed self-love and self-sufficiency as survival techniques. Or they might have grown up with overinflated praise: *You're the best! You're gonna be a star! You're sooo brilliant and gifted! Good fucking job!* So the second they weren't "the best," they felt deeply slighted, almost victimized. To compensate for those feelings, their egos grew into masks of self-confidence.

Any way you slice it, people with dominant Egotist Imposters often have an impenetrable cage around their heart so that no one can hurt them. They attack before getting attacked. They don't just go out of their way to occupy center stage—they expect it, and they demand the spotlight.

THE SUPERPOWERS OF THE EGOTIST IMPOSTER

Having a dominant Egotist Imposter, however, is not entirely negative. A solid ego is a necessary part of self-confidence. Without an ego, we have fuzzy boundaries and lose ourselves in other people. We succumb to guilt, and we say yes when we should or want to say no. A healthy ego helps us maintain boundaries with emotional users like, well, narcissists!

That's why people with dominant Egotist Imposters who are self-actualized are often strong and self-possessed leaders, direct in their interaction with others, and even protective of others. Many of them are true trailblazers. When they empower people instead of intimidating them, they are remarkable change agents.

Accessing your Egotist Imposter can also help you creatively finesse your way out of challenging situations and even manifest new opportunities for yourself. Consider filmmaker Gina Prince-Bythewood. In an NPR interview, Prince-Bythewood told radio host Terry Gross how she overcame her incredible

> **People with dominant Egotist Imposters who are self-actualized are often strong and self-possessed leaders, direct in their interaction with others, and even protective of others. Many of them are true trailblazers. When they empower people instead of intimidating them, they are remarkable change agents.**

shyness and introversion to pitch movies to hard-ass Hollywood producers, who were mostly white men. How did she do that? Well, in her younger years Prince-Bythewood was a basketball star. The minute she stepped onto the court, she became a fearless badass who lost all her introversion and owned her power with self-confidence and pride. Say hello to the superpower of the Egotist Imposter. She told Gross that every time she walks into a Hollywood studio, she imagines that she is walking onto a basketball court. She literally channels her inner fierce warrior athlete. She disowns her Victim Imposter and lets the superpower energy of her warrior basketball athlete—or the transformative power of her Egotist Imposter—infuse her spirit.

I had a similar experience when I was starting out as an actress and had one of my first auditions. It was for a Japanese TV commercial for teriyaki burgers, and I was terrified. I had always viewed casting agents and producers as enemies who were keen on exposing my flaws before pressing the reject button. I was sure that they were hell-bent on crushing my spirit.

Worse, if I blew an audition, I thought my career would be over. A memo would be sent out to all of Hollywood: *Don't waste your time auditioning Lisa Haisha. She can't act.* This was the flip side of the Egotist Imposter at the reins, exposing all its insecurities and fears. So, with all that negative self-talk in my head, how do you think I did on that commercial audition in front of six Japanese businessmen and two hardened female casting directors from Los Angeles?

Well, I did everything wrong. I dressed too casually for the part. I put my hair in a ponytail when a more businesslike look would have been appropriate. And I was nervous—very nervous. I was supposed to pretend that I was eating my lunch: a big, delicious teriyaki burger. Then I had to have a quick phone chat while I kept taking bites of my juicy burger.

Sounds easy, right?

It wasn't. This was one of my first auditions, and I fumbled through the whole thing. I made up lame dialogue and tried (miserably) to enjoy my pretend burger. It was a relief at the end when I delivered my one-and-only line flawlessly: *"Oishii desu!"*

The stone-faced Japanese agents stared at me. I didn't even get a fake smile. The two casting agents quickly gave me a curt "thank you" and sent me on my way. In audition-speak, that translates more or less to this: *"You suck. Run, don't walk, out of here. And don't come back. Ever."*

I sped off and threw myself on my sofa back home. I was humiliated, mortified, and frustrated. My Egotist Imposter was having a field day. *You're a big phony loser, Lisa!* it said. *You can't even fake eating a hamburger, for fuck's sake.*

But have you ever had moments when you're so down that the only way left to go is up? That's what happened. In a moment of clarity, I thought, *Screw my Egotist Imposter. I'll flip it on its head and use it as a creative superpower.* I had nothing left to lose, so I summoned every ounce of self-confidence I could muster, determined to somehow get another crack at that audition. I needed to think outside the box and muster the *self-confidence* of the Egotist Imposter: I had to *visualize* myself actually getting the part.

So that's just what I did: I took my hair down, and I put on a black skirt and crisp white top. Then I looked in the mirror and said to myself and to my Egotist Imposter: *It's only fair that you get another chance at the audition, Lisa. You blew it this morning, but you want the job and you have the creative chops to make it happen. You know your craft. You can already see yourself on the big screen. Give yourself another shot. You'll nail it!*

I brought in a different headshot to the audition—a serious, more dramatic one. I put a muzzle on my Overthinker Imposter (more on that later) and went back to the agency pretending to be someone else. I arrived fifteen minutes before casting ended, filled out the forms again, and submitted my "dramatic" headshot. The assistant handed it to the two casting directors as the Japanese men looked me over. *We're fooling them,* my Egotist Imposter said confidently. I chuckled.

The Japanese men gave me the same instructions I'd heard earlier that morning. I hit my mark and did everything they told me to do. I flat-out nailed the whole routine. But then one of the casting agents looked me over—a little too closely, I thought. Confused, she said, "That was excellent. But don't we know you from somewhere? You look familiar."

"I work all the time," I replied. "You've probably seen me before."

The other casting agent flipped through the stack of photos on her desk, stopped at one, lifted it out of the stack, and raised it triumphantly. "Here it is!"

She put it next to my other photo. Then she showed it to me and her partner. "Isn't this the same?" she asked. "It's the same name—Lisa Haisha—but a different photo."

"Strange," I said, putting my finger to my lips and doing the best acting job of my life. (I was definitely in touch with the creative side of my Egotist Imposter now.) "Oh my God!" I shouted. "That must have been my twin sister! She wants to be an actress so badly, but she can't act her way out of a wet paper bag, and she can't afford headshots. I'm sure she was here . . ." (I do have a twin sister, but she had no desire to be an actress. She was an incredible photographer.)

The casting agents looked perplexed at first, then relented. "Ah yes, apparently she *was* here! So sorry about the confusion. We'll get back to you shortly." For the second time that day, I got the hell out of there as quickly as I could. When I got home, there was already a message on my phone that I got the job.

This was a great lesson for me: I could have let my Egotist Imposter convince me that I was worthless. In that case I probably would have ended up flipping burgers at a local dive, instead of acting in a commercial for burgers at a local TV studio. By harnessing the superpower of my Egotist Imposter, I was able to blaze through my limiting self-beliefs and create a new reality for myself.

We've all heard the adage that if you want to change your reality, you have to change your beliefs about yourself. That's easier said than done, I know. But harnessing the superpowers of the Egotist Imposter is one way to make shift happen.

THE S.O.U.L. OF THE EGOTIST IMPOSTER

Many people with dominant Egotist Imposters put on a good show, but they're actually in a lot of denial. The older we get, the more difficult it can be to blaze through the deeply rooted behaviors and habits of this Imposter. That was certainly the case for my SoulBlazing client Sean.

Sean was a middle-aged, formerly successful entrepreneur in the midst of an ugly divorce—his fourth. According to Sean, women made him the victim, fooling him into romantic relationships that inevitably turned into marriage. Then the women would "go psycho" on him. He came to me wanting to get his business back on track, but with all the drama in his current divorce, he couldn't focus and had really low energy.

"I keep marrying crazy women, and it's screwing up my business mojo," he said. "I can't be everywhere at once. In court, on-site, trying to take care of everybody else's problems. I employ a lot of people, and they aren't talented enough to handle the job without me. They depend on me, and if I don't start jacking up profits, people's kids go hungry. They don't have the marketing savvy I do, so everything falls on me. I need to clone myself to get back on my feet."

Sean was so busy projecting his woes onto other people that he didn't realize he sounded like a windbag. (Sorry, Sean.) The Egotist Imposter was clearly driving his relentless whining.

I suggested that he volunteer at a retirement home to assist elderly residents with their basic needs. Being of service would help him step out of his constant focus on himself. Naturally, he hated the idea. I might as well have suggested that he skydive in his underwear. But here's what I explained to him: giving to others is a simple yet profound way of stepping outside the vortex of your own personal issues and into a more purposeful, heartfelt relationship with the world at large. As author and motivational speaker Simon Sinek wisely put it, "If you want to feel happy, do something for yourself. If you want to feel fulfilled, do something for someone else."

> **Giving to others is a simple yet profound way of stepping outside the vortex of your own personal issues and into a more purposeful, heartfelt relationship with the world at large.**

Sean wasn't buying this at first. "Are you kidding?!" he shouted during our first session. It was quickly becoming his mantra. "I don't have time. My company depends on me to succeed! *You don't understand the stress I'm under!*" He leaned forward, looked me in the eye, and said, "I. Don't. Have. Time. Do you understand what that means?"

The only way to cut through the bombast was to do some S.O.U.L. work with Sean. I leaned closer to him and looked him straight in the eye. "Sean, can I talk with your Egotist Imposter for a minute?"

He stared at me with a twitch in his eye. "My what?"

"Your Egotist Imposter. I want you to drop your guard and do an exercise with me. First I need you to STOP all the chatter and resistance in your head and just sit with me quietly."

"OK," he said, not looking at all OK about it.

I held his hands, and we looked into each other's eyes for a few minutes until I felt Sean let down his guard. Without spelling it out, I was engaging in eye-gazing with him. Slowly but surely, he started to lose his edge. "What are you gaining from keeping barricades around your heart?" I finally asked when I felt him soften up.

He flinched. "Barricades around my heart?"

"Yes," I replied. "You seem resistant to helping people. You seem resentful."

"I just don't feel like it's my responsibility to help everyone. No one helped me. I am where I am because of *my* hard work and determination. I'm certainly not going to allow a few bimbo wives to take everything from me. And *I* don't think reading to the elderly helps anyone," he persisted. "It certainly doesn't help my employees, their families, or *my* bottom line."

"I get that," I replied, "but when you open your heart to others, incredible things happen. You start to see your world with more perspective. Right now, you think that your failed marriages are not your fault and your business associates are wrong, incapable of doing a job well themselves. But you chose them, right? That means you either chose the crazy ones or you drove them crazy."

He looked at me quizzically.

"So, which one is it, Sean?" I asked. "Maybe you chose wives and employees who needed you, who were crying out for rescue. You chose 'broken' people who you could control so that you could be the smartest person in the room. Does that sound like a possibility?"

He lowered his head in affirmation. Sean was starting to look back and OBSERVE his behavior. "Yeah, that might be the case. Possibly."

"How's that working out for you?"

He smiled at me as if to say: *OK, I get it.* I nodded. "A competent and together person would probably scare you," I continued. "You'd lose control. You'd be forced to trust them. And that's one thing you fear most in life: trusting people enough to let go, because you never had anyone you could trust growing up."

Suddenly Sean's gaze shifted. He had that deer-in-the-headlights look that told me I'd hit the spot. *Bingo!* I had zeroed in on Little Sean—that innocent kid who was once open to love before childhood emotional abuse took its toll. "I can see that Little Sean is easygoing, relaxed, and open to love," I said. "But you make that impossible. What do you need from Big Sean to allow him to experience love?"

Big Sean looked away from me. By awakening and embodying his childhood self, something was starting to shift in his adult self. Sure enough, his shoulders began to shake as he *really* let down his guard and started to cry. "My parents criticized me relentlessly. They never let up, and they never really connected with me on an emotional level. I always felt alone and unworthy of love—I still do." Sean looked back at me, eyes red-rimmed.

"What do you need from Little Sean?" I gently asked.

"I don't know," he said. After a few more moments of silence, he continued, "I need Little Sean to connect with me. To reassure me that he won't abandon me. I guess what I'm saying is that I need to find a way to reconnect to myself. I don't even know who the fuck I am deep down."

Big Sean was starting to UNDERSTAND that for most of his life, he'd tried to ignore the vulnerability of his Authentic Self—"Little Sean"—to avoid feeling pain.

I suggested that Sean start with baby steps and do some mirror work (see the "Tools and Exercises" part), putting Big Sean on the back burner and connecting with Little Sean. Eventually, Sean agreed to volunteer at a "special needs" event. He still didn't like the assignment, but to his credit, he did it. There he was supervised by a man who was clearly respected and loved by the people working for him.

For the first time in his life, Sean allowed himself to be out of his element, but he was still uncomfortable and bad-tempered. Finally, he begrudgingly asked for help from his volunteer supervisor. The man was loving and patient with Sean, teaching him about social services step-by-step and thoroughly answering all his questions. Sean was totally perplexed by the man's generosity of spirit. "Who *are* you?" he finally asked. "What do you do?"

By awakening and embodying his childhood self, something was starting to shift in his adult self.

The man explained that he spent a day each week volunteering for community projects. He had saved up enough money to purchase a truck, which he used to collect food from local restaurants. He cooked dinner for the homeless once a week in a local park. Afterward, he broke everything down and went back to his day job. Yes, his *day* job. Even though he had very little and was pressed for time in every aspect of his life (some months he could barely make his rent), the man was richer than Sean in his comparatively "successful" life. He understood that being of service to others takes you out of the smallness of your own issues and into the bigger realm of the heart. And that's because he found purpose and meaning in being of service to others.

Over time the experience humbled Sean. He became a different person. As we continued to do the S.O.U.L. work together—as Sean learned to STOP, OBSERVE, and UNDERSTAND his behavior—he was eventually able to LIBERATE himself from the unproductive nature of his Egotist Imposter and move into more real, loving, and fulfilling relationships with others. "If you empower people around you instead of intimidating them," I told him one day, "your life will shift immediately."

Sean eventually learned not to lunge into relationships that fed his Egotist Imposter's desire to find imperfections and faults in women as a way of protecting himself. Embracing his Authentic Self and volunteering for the sheer sake of doing good for others made Sean happier and more deeply connected to people. He no longer needed to get defensive or always be right.

Sean was also greatly served by the "Inventory of Hurts" exercise. (See the "Tools and Exercises" part.) He started asking himself what he really wanted in life, then ended with "Am I serving myself or others with this choice?" I've never seen an exercise more effective at pointing people in the right direction before making important decisions about how their choices affect everyone around them.

People with dominant Egotist Imposters are everywhere. You can't miss them, even if you try! But behind the bombast, there's a lot of emotional pain. The exercises in the last part of this book are designed to help us blaze through some of the pain so that we can get in touch with our Authentic Souls.

In the meantime, if the Egotist Imposter sounds familiar to you, then you'll probably be equally familiar with the Imposter in our next chapter. It's so similar to the Egotist Imposter that it's easy to confuse the two: they're both delightful and dangerous in equal measure.

A QUICK RECAP OF THE EGOTIST IMPOSTER

People with dominant Egotist Imposters are usually too busy talking about themselves to spend much time focusing on other people. They're often full of bombast, which is a front: they might act like they're Masters of the Universe, but in reality they're more like the Wizard of Oz behind his curtain with pulleys and levers, filled with insecurities.

Paradoxically, deep down, people with dominant Egotist Imposters often have *compromised* self-esteem, even though they seem to brim with self-love and self-centeredness. When our egos are wounded during childhood (or when our sense of self and self-acceptance is challenged), we develop defense mechanisms and emotional patterns that emerge as a dominant Egotist Imposter within.

The Superpower: *Bold, charismatic, confident*
The Saboteur: *Insensitive, self-centered, unempathetic*

THE
SEDUCTOR

CHAPTER 5

THE SEDUCTOR

*I'm not trying to be sexy. It's
just my way of expressing
myself when I move around.*

—Elvis Presley

S ex sells. So what's new? That's been the case ever since Cleopatra put on black eyeliner and seduced the entire kingdom of Egypt. We all adore seductors because they're so, well, seductive. And the list of famous lovers and seductors of all genders is so long that it could fill this entire book. It's the stuff of cinema and literature. It's the first time we fall in love and our last heartbreak.

But for starters, let's not confuse sexuality with seduction. Sexuality is directly related to sex and physical sensuality. A vibrant, healthy sexuality is unrivaled in its beauty. It's the source of the delicate shapes of flowers and the vibrant hues of birds. As Marilyn Monroe reminded us, "Sex is a part of nature." Sexual energy created us and ushered us into the world.

Seduction, on the other hand, is a mindset. It's about beguiling people, drawing them into your presence, luring, and tantalizing. It's therefore no surprise that on a very basic level, the primary motive of people with dominant Seductor Imposters is to influence others through overt charm or more discreet game playing. The former is often called flirtation. The latter is called manipulation.

If you have a dominant Seductor Imposter, you're probably a pro at flattering people and luring them into your web through false feelings of intimacy, whether those feelings are sexual or emotional. Maybe you do that by charming people and using your own physical charm: you've read every book about how to become a world-class seductor. But here's a little secret: ironically, people with dominant Seductor Imposters might seem to *crave* intimacy—they certainly draw people into their orbit with the promise of it—but what actually animates them behind the scenes is *fear* of it.

Why is that the case?

Well, to experience real intimacy (not the fake kind), you need to feel safe: safe to open up and share genuine feelings. Safe to be seen and received by another person. Safe to be touched, whether that touch is emotional or physical. But to feel safe, you need trust. And if you grew up without it—if you grew up, in other words, feeling unsafe—chances are high that you're going to have a hard time experiencing intimacy.

But listen up: that doesn't mean you won't *crave* it. All human beings do, whether it's emotional or physical. "No other form of communication is as universally understood as touch," writes author Randi Fine. And no other form of communication is as universally healing, I might add. So you might crave intimacy, but if you grew up feeling unsafe or not able to trust key figures in your life, you'll struggle with it.

Maybe you were abused as a child or young adult. Or you had a promiscuous parent and grew up thinking that seduction and sex are the only ways to get love and attention. On the flip side, maybe your parents were controlling and super restrictive; maybe they never showed any form of intimacy, or worse, they vilified it. You grew up thinking intimacy was somehow "bad." But you know what they say about "bad" things: if you make something forbidden, it's exactly what you end up craving.

Whichever way you slice it, when the Seductor Imposter is in the driver's seat, people often jump from relationship to relationship, deflecting attention from themselves to others because, since they never felt safe or trusting, they don't have the self-confidence to build long-lasting ties. Their seductive charm actually masks this insecurity and low self-esteem. The lower the self-esteem, in fact, the more frenetic their search for prey becomes—and the more of a player they appear to be, fomenting jealousy and leaving hurtful drama in their wake.

In romantic situations (in the bedroom, to be specific), they might be absolutely fabulous, but they also tend to fixate on how their body looks and performs (never mind getting their own pleasure) versus bringing their partner pleasure or experiencing authentic intimacy. They have a lot of passion but not a lot of love. ("Don't confuse passion with love," a wise friend used to tell me.) So once a situation or romantic partner has been "conquered," they inevitably lose interest and can throw their partner under the bus without batting an eye. Then they seek their next prey.

THE SUPERPOWERS OF THE SEDUCTOR IMPOSTER

The Seductor Imposter definitely has its superpowers, of course: charm, charisma, zeal, and spontaneity. People with dominant Seductor Imposters create great social environments because they're tapped into sensuality at a high level and entertaining, which makes people feel good in their presence. They're the best kind of bon vivant. When they've done their emotional house-keeping, people with dominant Seductor Imposters can be

The Seductor Imposter definitely has its superpowers, of course: charm, charisma, zeal, and spontaneity.

brilliant partners: pleasure-seeking and compassionate sensualists who are good at forging deep connections.

And when they finally have big moments of self-actualization, they can quickly transform their lives in surprising ways. This was the case with my client Jonathan, a handsome fortysomething executive who played his seduction game with ruthless efficiency.

Here's what Jonathan's modus operandi was all about: he would gain a woman's trust with engaging, thoughtful conversation and false flattery, lure her into the bedroom, and shortly thereafter ghost her. (Yes, the online date from hell.) He was most often drawn to women he could lord over with his professional power, promising them some sort of job opportunity if they slept with him. If that woman was part of his professional circle (and that was often the case), he'd dangle a carrot in front of her: if you want this promotion, he'd suggest, you're gonna have to work *hard* for it behind closed doors. That's code for sex, in case I'm being too subtle.

Sound familiar?

This was basically standard behavior in so many circles before the #MeToo movement brought it out of the closet and the long-overdue process of condemnation began. Not that it's over, but at least progress has been made. In any case, when Jonathan first came into my office, he embodied the Seductor Imposter at its worst. "It's *sooo* easy to fuck anyone in this town," he crowed, sprawled carelessly across my counseling couch. Then he went on to relate conquest after conquest until I stopped him.

Jonathan was clearly so wrapped up in his own neurosis that subtlety wasn't going to work. I needed to channel my inner Mathena and get right in his face.

"All right, I get it," I said, signaling with my hand for him to stop. "Always a straight-up transaction. And guess what happens next, after you take advantage of a vulnerable woman's trust? She falls apart." I then told him about the many women who came into my office after dealing with dominant Seductor Imposter types like him: their lives were ruined by the emotional abuse, the sexual compromises woven into the deception of it all. "You're basically a dream crusher who abuses women's trust and shatters their fragile self-esteem."

I knew this firsthand as an actress in Hollywood. The bigger the roles I was offered, the more often I was asked by male directors to compromise my values by "performing services" (yes, please read between the lines). This was before the #MeToo movement, when men like Jonathan were a dime a dozen and got away with Very Bad Behavior. It was the norm. They dashed dreams and filled countless women with pent-up rage.

A silver lining was waiting at the end of my own encounters with out-of-control Hollywood Seductor Imposters: disgusted by this behavior and confused about who I truly was, I ditched everything and set out to my father's homeland in war-torn Iraq to discover my roots. This set me on a life-changing, SoulBlazing path.

I decided not to spare Jonathan the details of my experiences with men who insisted that I "show some skin" (among other things) to further my acting career. Jonathan stared at me, speechless. I had stopped him in his tracks by obliging him to see his own behavior mirrored in my experiences. After a moment of silence, I leaned forward and smiled. "So if you're finally ready to get real, shall we do a little exercise?"

THE S.O.U.L. OF THE SEDUCTOR IMPOSTER

Our first step in that exercise, as you may have guessed, was to STOP. I asked Jonathan to sit back, take a deep breath, and close his eyes. We were both going to sit quietly and get centered. But Jonathan was annoyed. "Are we going to meditate? Because I don't meditate. That's not my thing."

"This is not about formal meditation," I explained. "It's about simply getting quiet inside."

"I *am* quiet inside," he protested.

"Trust me," I replied. "You're not."

Jonathan rolled his eyes and resigned himself to the process. He sat back, closed his eyes, and started to focus on his breathing. Within a few minutes, I could sense a notable change in him: his energy seemed calm, and his face softened.

"So, Jonathan," I began. "I'm going to ask you an important question. Why do you need to stand on other people to elevate your own self-worth?"

He was quiet for a moment, then sheepishly admitted that he often sinks into a depression. "The only way I can feel better is to track down a woman and, you know, get intimate with her. But then I lose interest. So then I need to track down a new one."

"Say hello to your Seductor Imposter."

"My what?"

I went on to describe the traits of this archetype and told him that to get to the root of his depression, we needed to do some improv and journey back to his past. During our sessions Jonathan had spoken briefly about his mother, a distant woman who drank heavily to hide from the pressures of a harsh reality. Jonathan was an only child. And as a single mother, she'd had a hard time providing for them both economically, so they drifted from town to town in search of stability that never came. Meanwhile, she found so much solace in booze that she went from being a heavy drinker to an alcoholic. It was time for Jonathan to revisit his past and OBSERVE the nature of his Seductor Imposter to UNDERSTAND how it might have been formed during this critical time in his past.

"Let's talk about your mother," I told him. "Let's go deeper and consider how you two might have influenced each other."

Taking my cues from active improvisation, I *became* his mother and role-played her. One moment I was the worrying nurturer. The next moment I was a young mother with her whole life ahead of her—if she could only get away from the child who held her back. I amped up the intensity of each confrontation, channeling the woman's fear, anger, and sense of betrayal.

"You ruined my life!" I shouted. "If I'd never had you, men would stay with me and I'd be happy." I kept screaming at him while I edged my way out of my chair. "Because of you, I have no money. Because of you, I have no life!"

"Oh my God," he whispered, stunned by the revelation. He realized that on some level, his mother had blamed him for the men who dumped her—and that he had internalized that blame. And what rhymes with blame? Shame. That's what coursed through Little Jonathan when he was a kid: shame. He came to the devastating conclusion that he'd been unconsciously getting back at his mother for the shame he internalized by destroying the lives of the young women who looked to him to advance their careers.

In creating a space for Jonathan to OBSERVE this dynamic, he was able to UNDERSTAND himself better. Our role-playing had touched his Authentic Soul.

"I don't want to be *anything* like my mother," he said.

Next in store for Jonathan was a SoulBlazing exercise I call "Into the Looking Glass" (see the "Tools and Exercises" part). This exercise helped him come to grips with the depth of his sub-conscious self-pity—how he'd learned to view himself as a victim, held back by his emotionally brutal upbringing.

Jonathan's Seductor Imposter justified treating women like trash because his mother had treated him like trash. And since people like Jonathan would rather leave someone than find himself abandoned, he jumped from partner to partner. It was only when Jonathan was able to STOP, OBSERVE, and UNDERSTAND this pattern that he was able to slowly LIBERATE himself from its vise grip.

The key to keeping this Imposter in check is harnessing the passion of its creativity, rather than using it as a mask that ultimately creates pain and drama. And people who have dominant Seductor Imposters aren't always men. Not long after I first arrived back in Los Angeles after my solo global travels, I was invited to attend the Emmy Awards with a boyfriend. It was a landmark moment for our relationship. I wanted to make a great impression with a smashing red-carpet look, so I spent hours prepping for the big night, from fresh polish on my toes to carefully styled hair. I was ready to take my place among the stars.

On that special night, my boyfriend arranged for a limo to pick me up at my apartment, then drive out to Malibu to pick up Sharon, the wife of his partner. My boyfriend and his partner were both nominated for an award that evening. As I was whisked out of Los Angeles down the Pacific Coast Highway, past one multimillion-dollar home after another, I began to worry: I would soon be joined by a former A-list actress, a face everybody in the country would recognize. Was I pretty enough? Was I glam enough? Did I deserve to be among the rich and famous? These questions morphed into a sinking feeling that only deepened as we pulled up in front of her house.

Gliding out the front door and down the cobblestone walkway came a slinky blonde with jaw-dropping curves. She wore an elegant but simple black gown, and her hair flowed freely in the breeze. Envy and self-consciousness immediately consumed me. Feeling overly coiffed, I wondered why her hair wasn't in a fancy updo. *Isn't that how all women wear their hair at awards ceremonies?* That was my little-girl voice from my Middle Eastern upbringing talking, I realized later.

Sharon slid into the seat next to me and hiked up her gown. Slipping a cell phone into the top of her thigh-high stocking, she nonchalantly revealed an intimate part of her anatomy. "What are you doing?" I asked her, taken aback by the casualness of the gesture.

"I don't want to carry a big purse," she said. Her voice was flat and unemotional. She was stunning despite minimal makeup. I felt nervous and intimidated. I was about to put on my Seductor Imposter mask to be hip and mirror her.

"Your hair looks pretty simple," I said, suddenly feeling over-dressed and insecure.

"This was the best I could do," she said, her limp wave imply-ing that she had spent about five minutes getting ready for the evening. "I had two choices: put on some lip gloss and eyeliner and get in the limo, or stay home and shoot myself."

In the silence that followed, it became clear that she wasn't exaggerating. My Seductor Imposter was initially on overdrive around her, but I realized that I could remove my own mask and simply be me. I suddenly felt compassion, not envy, for this exotic creature. "I don't know what your situation is," Sharon went on, "but I go from one event to another being arm candy for my hus-band. I can't remember who I am. Maybe I'm a living blow-up doll, I suppose. I want to quit this whole business and just leave, maybe travel." She paused. "I'm just so sick of it all."

For most people—including me—a trip to an awards show was a fantasy come true. For Sharon, an evening on the town was a mandatory part of her relationship with her husband. It was just another job to complete. She had spent the last decade mak-ing connections, networking, and attending dinner parties and Hollywood's biggest events, but no one cared who she was any-more. She had slowly lost contact with her Authentic Self and her Authentic Soul. (Actress Liv Ullmann once said that Hollywood was "loneliness beside the swimming pool." She wasn't far off.)

All of a sudden it struck me as ironic: There I was, in front of this beauty with wealth and fame, envying her sexiness, her life, and its trappings. And yet just fifteen minutes into the evening, I discovered that *she* envied *me* when she asked me what I do.

"I travel and do volunteer work in developing countries," I told her. "I'm writing a book about my experience in orphanages around the world called *Whispers from Children's Hearts.*"

"I love developing countries," she said. "I'm sick of dressing up all the time and obsessing about staying a size 2 for people I don't really care about."

"So why don't you just do it? Why not pack it up and travel? You can come with me on my trip in the next few weeks."

"I can't. I have to go to engagements every week and host parties. I'm tethered to my husband. I have no other life."

Sharon, of course, *did* have a choice. In that moment I realized that when you live a false life, regardless of how glamorous it might seem, you won't find happiness or personal fulfillment.

The Seductor Imposter is tricky. If unchecked, it fuels all sorts of obsessive behaviors that lead to intense shame. We sometimes even end up weighed down with shameful secrets that come to define us in self-defeating ways. We can even become love junkies.

Take Jessica, an attorney with a shameful secret. From all outward appearances, she had everything. Beautiful in a classy, almost regal sort of way, she was a true Washington insider. She worked with the United Nations, routinely made appearances at swank VIP political events, and was well respected in her field. She seemed in absolute control of every aspect of her life.

But three sessions into our work together, this facade cracked. I realized that Jessica was tormented more deeply than most. In her late twenties, she had engaged in all sorts of edgy sex, including orgies. "I enjoy the extreme danger of giving myself over to strangers," she said. "It's addictive. I crave the contact. Anonymous sex consumes my thoughts."

She admitted that she was powerless over her impulsive sex drive. The Seductor Imposter was woven deep into the tapestry of her life. But now, as her political job put her more in the spotlight, her taboo behavior morphed into a secret shrouded in intense shame. Her life would unravel if her exploits were ever revealed to the public. "I've managed to keep a rein on everything else in my life and in my career," she admitted, "but I've never been able to kick the shame of my past."

Jessica and I engaged in the S.O.U.L. exercise. As we worked together, Jessica spoke about her past for the first time. Born into a family with a traditional culture, she had always felt alienated. Both parents had been born and raised in Iran. She learned early that sex was a sin, and that you had sex with your husband only to have children. After you were finished making babies, there was no more sex for the women. (But for men? A different story!)

> **When you live a false life, regardless of how glamorous it might seem, you won't find happiness or personal fulfillment.**

"I was born into the wrong family, the wrong city, the wrong country, to parents living in the wrong century," she told me, shrugging her shoulders. *What's a person supposed to do?* As a teenager and into her early twenties, Jessica rebelled against her family's restrictions by using Ecstasy, which loosened her up sexually, taking her out of her head and into her body. The exhilaration became a craving. Then she met people with whom she sought even bigger thrills.

"I can just imagine it now," she said, referring to her past in light of her present, which included being nominated for a judgeship. "In the middle of a press conference, some reporter might ask me: 'Judge, can you confirm or deny the claims that you participated in orgies?'"

"That could happen," I conceded.

This woman, full of compassion and intelligence, was one indiscreet comment away from losing everything. To her credit, Jessica blazed through the walls she had built around her Authentic Soul. She went into therapy to work on herself and eventually understood how she had succumbed to her parents' values rather than her own. She stopped betraying and punishing herself as she stepped more fully into her own power, practicing self-forgiveness and avoiding the high-stress public arena. And to her great credit, she shifted her focus from sexuality to sensuality: she took up pole dancing (a lot safer than promiscuous relationships with strangers) and perfected her belly dancing. In fact, she wanted to become a belly-dancing teacher.

I shared with Jessica how I'd shifted my own goals when I released my budding acting career to seek more meaningful work traveling and studying, which eventually led to my work in psychology and life coaching. I encouraged her to rethink the nature of her anxiety-producing job, where she was constantly afraid of "getting caught."

Jessica slowly came to terms with the fact that she could not run for higher office, so she found other ways to fulfill her ambitions, like painting and other artistic pursuits. She began a meditation practice and focused on staying in the present, on "just being." Then she quit her prestigious job. Her demons still occasionally rose up, but meditation had taught her how to visualize putting each "demon" on a leaf that floated to the ground. She also came clean with one of her sisters, who later became her rock: supportive and understanding of what Jessica was going through, her sister embraced her in all her beautiful imperfections.

The takeaway here is simple: If we ignore the dark side of this Imposter, it can drive us down all sorts of self-destructive rabbit holes. But when we implement the S.O.U.L. practice in a sincere commitment to self-awareness, we're able to harness the super-powers of the Seductor Imposter and make meaningful shifts happen, since the positive energy of this Imposter is powered by charisma, passion, and fervor for life.

A QUICK RECAP OF THE SEDUCTOR IMPOSTER

The primary motive of people with dominant Seductor Imposters is to influence others through overt charm or more discreet game playing. (The former is often called flirtation. The latter is called manipulation.)

People with dominant Seductor Imposters are often pros at flattering people and luring them into their web through false feelings of intimacy. But here's a little secret: ironically, people with dominant Seductor Imposters might seem to *crave* intimacy—and they draw people into their orbit with the promise of it. But what actually animates them behind the scenes is *fear* of it.

The Superpower: *Passionate, sensual, pleasure-driven*
The Saboteur: *Manipulative, secretive, sly*

THE
JOKER

CHAPTER 6

THE JOKER

I think of myself as an intelligent, sensitive human being with the soul of a clown which always forces me to blow it at the most important moments.

—Jim Morrison[3]

3. Jim Morrison, interview by Salli Stevenson, *Circus*, October 3, 1970, *The Doors: The Lost Interview Tapes*, volume two, CD-ROM.

The best way to start this chapter is probably with a joke, but God only knows which one. If you do a quick Google search on "best jokes of all time," you'll find jokes about death, hunters, dogs, little old ladies, drunks, gas station bathrooms, soup, sex, escalators, the state of Texas, secret agents, huts on secret islands, pirates, pancakes, and just about every religious denomination. And if you're dominant Imposter is the Joker, I'll bet you know them all. (Did you notice that I've spared you even one joke in this first paragraph? You're welcome.)

Everyone has a friend, family member, or coworker who's quick with a joke in any situation. That person is often the life of the party. But people who use humor pathologically—well, that's different. It's seriously not funny. A wall of constant jokes is precisely that: a wall. It's hiding something that's probably not very funny. Like (I'm sure you guessed it) deep-seated insecurities and emotional pain.

The Joker is a powerful archetype: They are the jester, the dunce, the trickster, and the shape-shifter. They are the ones who hide their despair behind the theatrical smile of the clown, sometimes in the extreme. No wonder clowns are often depicted as freaky-scary in movies! The duality of your classic clown with a forced smile is creepy: happy and entertaining on the one hand, miserable on the other. But we can't seem to get enough of these archetypes: Joaquin Phoenix gave us all a look at the agony behind the clown makeup and the emptiness behind the laughter in *Joker*.

Joker Imposters usually develop when people who had difficult childhoods use humor to survive. Often they were not seen or heard much, and they had to deal with deprivation and anger issues in the family while growing up. If that's you, then you probably used humor to deflect emotions by entertaining and distracting people, which developed a hard shell around your heart so that no one could hurt you. But if humor protects you, it also distances you from real, authentic relationships.

> **If you have a dominant Joker Imposter, you might desperately want to belong but end up sabotaging the very intimacy you crave.**

Laughter is important, but humor can wrongly be used at the expense of others, as Cyndi Sarnoff-Ross, a licensed psychotherapist, explains. She goes on to suggest that people who use humor as their default mode are often "defending against their own insecurities" about showing their true self in relationships.[4]

I've known countless people with dominant Joker Imposters, including one of my closest friends. She and I have had spats over

4. Courtney Howard, "Psychology Behind Defense Mechanisms: Using Humor to Cope (Part 4 of 4)" (blog post), Sovereign Health of California, October 16, 2015, https://www.sovcal.com/mental-health/psychology -behind-defense-mechanisms-humor-cope-part-4-of-4/.

her expert ability to turn anything into a joke at another person's expense. She'd call out people in front of others and sometimes betray a confidence by sharing what the average person would consider personal. But her Joker Imposter compelled her to shrug things off and say, "You never told me I couldn't say that."

If you have a dominant Joker Imposter, you might desperately want to belong but end up sabotaging the very intimacy you crave. In fact, you might actually care more than others about intimacy, but you've been so emotionally wounded in the past that you don't trust love or connection.

Despite their outward devil-may-care appearance, deep down, people with dominant Joker Imposters tend to be nervous, anxious, and overly concerned about impressing others. Sometimes they're intentionally rude to suggest that they don't give a damn, which is just insecurity masquerading as bravado. And while people with dominant Joker Imposters love being the center of attention, they are also deathly afraid of disappointing others. Thus, they constantly entertain in the hopes of endearing themselves to the group or to an individual they admire, preferably from a stage.

TEARS OF A CLOWN

No surprise: there is often a big disconnect between the roles that actors play and the real people behind the masks. History is filled with tales of actors who seemingly had it all, only to tumble down the rabbit hole of drug or alcohol addiction, or voluntarily end their lives. Some of these people were beloved comedians with keen Joker Imposters at their emotional helm.

The tale of Robin Williams is a perfect example. This universally loved entertainer, with his razor-sharp wit and hilarious antics, brought some of our most endearing characters to life on the big screen. But underneath his comic persona, Williams struggled with profound emotional pain, depression, and insecurity while growing up. He turned to drugs to ease his suffering and eventually became an addict. Even as he enthralled us with his irreverent humor, the dark shadow of his Joker Imposter brought him down. The world was deeply shocked when he ended his own life. How could such a seemingly lighthearted, zany comedian harbor such darkness?

In the 2018 biography *Robin*, author Dave Itzkoff calls Williams "an illusionist"; his magic trick was all about "making you see what he wanted you to see—the act and not the artist delivering it. Behind all the artifice, all the accents and characters, all the blurs of motion and flashes of energy, there was just a lone man facing the crowd, who decided which levers to pull and which buttons to press, which voices and facades to put on, how much to reveal and how much to keep hidden."

Itzkoff hits the nail on the head here: behind the "facade"— that is, the Joker Imposter—there's a lone man (or woman) facing a crowd—and a scared one too. If Williams had committed to sustained personal and spiritual work on the pain that fed his Joker Imposter, he might have learned to convert pain into a positive catalyst for change. That's precisely what another comedian did with his dominant Joker Imposter.

THE SUPERPOWERS OF THE JOKER IMPOSTER

Like Williams, Jim Carrey is a Hollywood icon. In his biography *The Joker Is Wild: The Trials and Triumphs of Jim Carrey*, author Martin Knelman describes how Carrey grappled with emotional complexities as a child. Carrey's father lost his job when Carrey was a young kid, leaving everyone homeless. The entire family had to clean out a factory at night as barter for lodging, which fueled Carrey's rage. An angry high school dropout later in life, Carrey was determined to rise above the insecurities of his childhood using comedy as a salve and a weapon.

As he rose through the ranks of the comedy world (starting, as most people do, at the bottom), his turbocharged Joker Imposter eventually helped him pave the way to incredible success as a world-class actor and comedian. It took years for him to work through the vagaries of his Joker Imposter, and there were days when Carrey felt bereft and emotionally lost. But he persevered: Among other feats of personal transformation, Carrey famously worked on the powers of visualization and wrote himself a $10 million check for "acting services rendered" when he was nearly broke. Ten years later he made $10 million after he was cast in the movie *Dumb and Dumber.*

As Dave Itzkoff quotes from an unknown provenance: "The creative adult is the child who survived." That was *literally* the case in the world of Ahmed Albasheer, an Iraqi comedian who is the Jon Stewart of the Arab world. Albasheer was a teenager in Baghdad during the shock-and-awe military campaign, when allied forces were bombarding the city and radical jihadists were rampant in the streets. One day at the height of that conflict, he was listening to the Backstreet Boys on his Walkman when his ultrareligious father walked through the door and went ballistic. For a religious Muslim, listening to Western pop music was a sin, so his father kicked him out of the house—literally.

"There was a massacre going on outside," Albasheer explained in the 2019 documentary *Larry Charles' Dangerous World of Comedy.* "But my father said, 'Go out! You're not a good Muslim boy—you're an infidel!'" Albasheer ended up being taken hostage by soldiers and sent to prison, but he avoided torture by making jokes that cracked up the security guards. Comedy writer Larry Charles included Albasheer and other people who used humor in some of the most violent parts of the world as a way to survive.

Talk about using the superpower of the Joker Imposter! This Imposter is often creative, fun, and wickedly smart.

THE S.O.U.L. OF THE JOKER IMPOSTER

Living in the heart of La-La Land, I've encountered more Joker Imposters than the average bear. Take Sahib. One of my BFFs was married to him. Sahib had an incorrigible dominant Joker Imposter at play at all times: anytime he saw me, Sahib would bombard me with his stale jokes. "Helloooo, Lisa!" he'd pipe up as soon as he'd see me. "Say, did you hear the one about the . . . ?" By the time he was done I'd want to turn around and go home.

A production designer by trade, Sahib was a relentless jokester everywhere he went. When he could keep his Joker Imposter in check, he was good at his job, but that wasn't often: he alienated most people at work almost immediately. On set Sahib would launch into long-winded (and sometimes offensive) jokes that no one but him found funny. At best, his clowning around was a distraction in the workplace. At worst, he was fired more than once for being inappropriate. His Joker Imposter was pathological, out of control.

After dealing with a number of setbacks at work, Sahib decided to see me in a professional context. He immediately zeroed in on his pathological joking as a source of discomfort to others. "I've really tried to refrain from telling jokes," he said during our first session. "But I've always had a problem taking things seriously. When I'm working, I come home irritated and tense. Humor's the only thing that really keeps me going."

It was time for Sahib to do a little S.O.U.L. work and get to the emotional roots behind all his stale wisecracking.

I asked Sahib to STOP, and we began the process of eye-gazing. Slowly but surely I could feel Sahib sink into a calmer, more serene state. When I felt he was truly centered and his Joker Imposter was in the back seat, I dived right in.

"Do you feel safe at home?" I asked.

"No," he said, looking down. "I don't feel safe with anyone."

"Well, who can you get real with?" I gently asked. "Who can you comfortably show your true self to?"

"My mom," he replied after a long beat. "I loved her. She always had my back. But she passed away when I was just a kid. I lived with my dad after that. He would yell at me, smack me around now and then."

"Did you humor him when he did that?"

Sahib was silent for a moment, then his eyes widened. "Actually, yeah. I never thought about that before. But to deflect his anger, I'd joke around. I'd goof off. I'd try to make him laugh."

I continued to push Sahib to explore moments when humor became a way of masking or thwarting emotional pain. And there were plenty—sad moments when Little Sahib tried to calm his irrational father with jokes. "I became a great impersonator," he told me. "I'd impersonate characters from movies or from TV. That always made my dad pause when he was in a rage."

Sure enough, Sahib started to OBSERVE the many ways he had hidden his Authentic Self behind the mask of humor to avoid being derided or hurt. It was a moment of awakening: he was able to OBSERVE the realities that shaped him as a child and created self-limiting behaviors that fed his Joker Imposter.

As we spoke about the abuse and bullying he suffered in his youth, I felt truly connected to Sahib and genuinely liked him. I finally saw his Authentic Soul through the Joker Imposter mask. I understood Sahib and sympathized with him, but more importantly, Sahib began to UNDERSTAND himself.

"From now on I want you to see your mother in others," I told him, drawing on the only source of strength and security he had ever known. "Especially when you're uncomfortable or tense, remember your mother's grace. Remember how she loved you and nurtured you."

He nodded.

"I want you to be that person for yourself. Stand up for yourself. You don't have to be 'on' to be liked and valued. As you can see, when you try too hard to be liked, it has the opposite effect."

From that session onward, Sahib tried to treat everyone as if they were his mom, from the folks he worked with to the cashier at the grocery store. He tried to harness the power of love and treat himself the way his mom had treated him as well. It wasn't easy: How can you treat your rude boss like they were your loving mother? Or the guy with road rage who cuts you off on the freeway? Or the so-called friend who betrays you? But Sahib persisted.

In their 2012 book *The Tools*, authors Phil Stutz and Barry Michels explore a tool they call "Active Love," which describes how tapping into the higher force of love is empowering enough to offset reactions like anger and rage. They call it "Outflow," which changes your inner state and ultimately gives you the freedom to respond rather than react. You end up "with more than you had when you began. Unlike water, if your glass is half-filled with love and you give it to your enemy to drink, the glass will return to you full" of love after he drinks it.

By tapping into the power of love that he felt from his mother, Sahib slowly began to take control of his Joker Imposter. He was able to respond rather than react to experiences that he perceived as emotional threats, without resorting to the defense mechanism of jokes and sarcasm. He was thus able to not only OBSERVE and UNDERSTAND his Joker Imposter but also LIBERATE himself from it as well.

We all love Jokers—to a point—because we all love to be entertained. Laughter is a salve. It's the best medicine around. Poet Pablo Neruda called it "the language of the soul." I know this to be a universal truth because I've seen this play out in every culture around the world. People find respite and release in laughter.

But laughter can also become a shield that masks a darker shadow. That's when the Joker Imposter is tripping us up. I've mentored countless people whose Joker Imposters got the best of them. They all used humor to deflect pain, which hindered their personal growth. It got in the way of their personal and professional relationships. It was emotionally draining. But once they mined the depths of what was under their pathological humor— in other words, once they wiped that Joker smile off their faces and took a good hard look at themselves—they all had major aha moments that led to huge transformations: more creativity, deeper engagement with life, and a lot more authentic fun. And that, dear readers, is no joke.

A QUICK RECAP OF THE JOKER IMPOSTER

The Joker Imposter is the jester, the dunce, the trickster, and the shape-shifter. People with dominant Joker Imposters often hide their despair behind the theatrical smile of the clown, sometimes in the extreme: they can be happy and entertaining one moment, and miserable the next.

Those with Joker Imposters at the helm desperately want to belong but end up sabotaging the very intimacy they crave. They're often so emotionally wounded that they don't trust love or connection, so they turn everything into a joke. That's a form of insecurity masquerading as bravado, even if it gets a laugh.

The Superpower: *Creative, adventurous, life of the party*
The Saboteur: *Insecure, wounded, duplicitous*

CHAPTER 7

THE FIXER

Knowledge of the self is the mother of all knowledge. So it is incumbent on me to know my self, to know it completely, to know its minutiae, its characteristics, its subtleties, and its very atoms.

—Kahlil Gibran, *The Treasured Writings of Kahlil Gibran*, 2013

Holy shit, there's a lot to fix out there. Where do we start? We need to "fix" climate change and socio-economic injustices. We need to "fix" our relationships with friends, partners, parents, kids, and colleagues. And we're constantly being told, either through advertising or other people's judgments—*or through our own tireless, self-critical Judge (see "The Judge" chapter)*—that we need to "fix" ourselves: we need to "self-improve" and "fix" our bodies, our mindsets, our lifestyles.

Are you exhausted yet?

The majority of us are aware that we should or could be fixing *some*thing. But those of us with dominant Fixer Imposters are aware of it chronically, almost pathologically. Because for those of us with this well-intentioned Imposter in the driver's seat, "fixing" things—whether it's ourselves or other people—is often as much a desire to make things better as it is a need to control things or exert dominance over others. And that's when this Imposter shifts from positive to negative and is at war with itself. Recall the two diametrically opposed brothers Alan and Charlie Harper in *Two and a Half Men*, and you get the picture.

For starters, you know the kind of people I'm talking about: they're the ones who always give you unsolicited advice. Key word here: "unsolicited." These people don't wait for you to ask them for help; whether you need it or not, they are always doling out their counsel about things. They might give advice about small things, like a nagging micromanaging parent does, or big things, like the person who creates an entire "Reinvention Life Plan" for their depressed friend, only to find that it sends their friend spiraling deeper into depression. Either way, under the guise of being helpful, these people can be overbearing, overearnest, and overwhelming.

THE SUPERPOWERS OF THE FIXER IMPOSTER

Before we get in too deep here, let's step back and start with the obvious: a Fixer Imposter is that part of our nature that wants to fix things. This is a good thing! In fact, the superpower of people with dominant Fixer Imposters is that they are tirelessly solution-oriented and helpful, particularly when the going gets rough. Famous TV personality Fred Rogers once said, "When I was a boy and would see scary things in the news, my mother would say to me, 'Look for the helpers. You will always find people who are helping.'"

Who doesn't want to find people who are always helping? Every day it seems like there's a crisis that needs urgent care. The world is always desperate for fixers, helpers, volunteers, and heartfelt agents of change. And in this context, people with dominant Fixer Imposters are stars in the constellation of humanity. They are naturally of service to others. If there is any Imposter type more likely to take a proverbial broom and clean up our messy global village, it's the Fixer.

But if you have a dominant Fixer Imposter, that superpower comes with a twist: you can be such a giver that you end up giving away your own power. Some people work for free or do underpaid work and end up undermining their own jobs; others are so busy helping people that they put their own well-being and health on the back burner until they literally get sick.

Many people with dominant Fixer Imposters are extreme in another way: they generally drive people crazy because they can't help trying to fix them—whether it's a friend, family member, coworker, you name it—and they drive *themselves* crazy as well, because they apply the same flawed fix-it logic to themselves. They think they are never thin enough, rich enough, smart enough, ambitious enough, healthy enough, happy enough, fill-in-the-blank enough. (They're also classic self-help junkies, with an insatiable appetite for the latest lifestyle advice book, podcast,

> **The superpower of people with dominant Fixer Imposters is that they are tirelessly solution-oriented and helpful, particularly when the going gets rough. Famous TV personality Fred Rogers once said, "When I was a boy and would see scary things in the news, my mother would say to me, 'Look for the helpers. You will always find people who are helping.'"**

trend, or craze.) And behind the drive to improve, remediate, and counsel others—or "fix" themselves—there is often a subtle (and sometimes a not-so-subtle) desire to control the world around them.

How does this come to pass, and what's *really* behind the Fixer Imposter?

People with this dominant Fixer Imposter often grow up in emotionally messy households, either without much parental guidance (read: latchkey kids), with too *much* parental guidance (read: overprotected, sheltered kids), or in the worst case, with abusive parents. They might have grown up worried about imminent catastrophes, being abandoned, not looking "right" or "perfect" enough, or hiding family shame. Their worrying often expresses itself in "what if" scenarios, whether that what-if is commonplace (*What if I fail? What if people don't like me?*) or outlandish (*What if the moon pops out of its orbit and hurtles toward Earth? What if my coworkers are actually extraterrestrials from a rogue planet?*).

In other words, people with dominant Fixer Imposters can also be master worriers. They see adversity and disaster around every corner, even in benign situations. In the extreme they become "catastrophizers." Fixing becomes an unconscious way of preventing a "what if" from happening. It also shares a common border with the preoccupations of the Overthinker Imposter, but we'll get to that in another chapter.

As adults, these good-natured and sensitive souls learned that the only way to make sense of life was to create order in the disorder around them and try to "fix" things. (Hint: many things can't really be "fixed," nor do they need to be.) These well-intentioned people are often easy to spot. They're the ones who have something to say about "fixing" your work life, your love life, your friends, your home, your finances, your body—basically everything from the sublime to the ridiculous. But don't be fooled: behind the relentless counseling, there is often the desire to control things—and behind that, there is fear and worry.

Parents with dominant Fixer Imposters (who I believe are most parents) want the best for their children, and it's painful for them if they see their kids acting out or not staying focused on things they feel are beneficial to them. These parents can sometimes actually drive their kids in the *opposite* direction, which may explain why their children sometimes end up being thrill seekers or otherwise love to defy social conventions. I can say that with confidence, because I was one of those kids.

Parents do their best, and no one is perfect and escapes childhood unscathed. My sisters and I, all raised by the same parents, grew into adults who are wildly different from one other. Our parents cared a lot and had different core values, which made us second-guess advice from either one. They both wanted us all to be happy and have fewer struggles than they did. I guess they wanted to fix what might be before "what might be" even happened. How did that inform me later in life? Well, all I wanted to do was travel as far away as possible. I wanted to feel alive. I wanted to meet strangers who could teach me and show me other ways of thinking and being in the world. I wanted to meet all the authors from the books I read and create my own experiences to write about one day. I wanted to meet magical people who could transport my mundane existence into an odyssey worth living.

I adored Madonna in my youth because she was the antithesis of Miss Chaldean (my inner-conforming Middle Eastern prom queen). I craved her unapologetic self-expression. In an incredible twist of fate, my first boyfriend in LA was Madonna's keyboardist, and I immediately fell in with a glamorous Hollywood crowd. I rubbed elbows on a regular basis with A-list celebrities, Madonna among them. I even went to Madonna and Sean Penn's wedding at a Malibu estate, blinded by the megawattage of all those stars.

Even though I was as straight as a ruler compared to Madonna, I felt a kinship to her because we had some baseline similarities: we were both born in Detroit, migrated to California, had overbearing foreign fathers, went to Catholic schools, and were part of the same generation. The similarities stopped there, of course.

I was still a caterpillar struggling to break out of my cocoon. She was a wild butterfly.

One day I asked Madonna if she had any advice about personal freedom and getting in touch with your Authentic Self. She

> **Advertising and self-improvement dogma would have us all believe that if we work hard enough and tirelessly on mind/body/soul, we can not only achieve perfection but become our "best selves." But that's as much a myth as, say, the unicorn that lives in your backyard.**

was sitting on a bench, tying her shoelaces at the time, getting ready for a run. She paused and looked me squarely in the eyes. She told me about the importance of finding your own authentic voice and why that's so difficult when you grow up conforming to someone else's belief system or judgments. She shared about digging deep to figure out who you are and what your soul came here to express. Summing up everything, she said, "Here's my advice: travel, travel, travel—and travel *alone.*"

I took those words to heart and did just that.

In the ensuing years I traveled all over the world, from Asia to Africa, from Europe to the Middle East. And I met every variety of human being under the sun. I eventually got my degree in spiritual psychology and became a life coach so that I could fix other people's problems for a living. Deep down, in part thanks to my parents' unconscious messaging and their own dominant Fixer Imposters, I grew into the risk-taking, world-traveling person that I am now. I did so partly in defiance of their constricting, protective rules. But I also developed a Fixer Imposter of my own.

That Fixer Imposter expresses itself in positive and negative ways. Like nearly every other woman on the earth, I grew up in a world filled with advertising predicated on convincing me that something was "wrong" with me that could be "fixed" with the latest cream, hair product, diet trend, fashion sensibility, lifestyle training—you name it. From your private parts to your inner thoughts, advertising is designed to prey on our insecurities—the Fixer Imposter's fodder.

This brings us to a dicey aspect of advertising that's traditionally been directed at women. (And yes, men are increasingly falling prey to advertising that was exclusively directed at women. How sad is that?) Advertising and self-improvement dogma would have us all believe that if we work hard enough and tirelessly on mind/body/soul, we can not only achieve perfection but become our "best selves." But that's as much a myth as, say, the unicorn that lives in your backyard.

The truth is that we're always our best selves, even when we're struggling with our personal demons. The idea here is not to become a manic overachiever or take our cues from other people whose journey might have nothing to do with our own. It's not about being your "best self," but rather about being truly yourself at your best. Author Karen Karbo explored this idea in her 2020 book, *Yeah, No. Not Happening.: How I Found Happiness Swearing Off Self-Improvement and Saying F*ck It All—and How You Can Too*. Karbo writes that your "best self" is "imaginary"—a social construct juiced by advertising designed to keep your Fixer Imposter busy "fixing" every possible "flaw" you might have. Taken to the extreme, this leads to body dysmorphic disorder (BDD), a new disorder that recently made its way into the *Diagnostic and Statistical Manual of Mental Disorders.* Karbo suggests that in addition to BDD, we should add BSDD, or what she calls "best-self dysmorphic disorder," which she describes as "the constant feeling that however 'good' we are, we are never enough.'"

People with superdominant Fixer Imposters not only internalize this message but also often inflict it on others. This leads to anxiety, depression, and confusion. We confuse our "best self" (a mirage that feeds our Fixer Imposter) with our *true* self, or our *Authentic Self.*

THE S.O.U.L. OF THE FIXER IMPOSTER

It goes without saying that the Fixer Imposter runs deep. When unchecked, it can sabotage your life. I've worked with all sorts of people in my SoulBlazing sessions whose Fixer Imposters fit that bill. Sarah, a fifty-year-old English beauty, is one of them.

Sarah bore three children out of wedlock when she was in her twenties. She worked multiple jobs at odd hours and all but abandoned her children so that she could make ends meet and provide for them. For a time, she became moderately successful against the odds, with a reputation as a well-respected physical fitness coach, a "star child" from a mean upbringing.

But Sarah had a problem: Even with the best of intentions, she came off as "preachy." She simply couldn't stop telling people what to wear, what to eat, how to act, and so on. And she didn't preach only to her clients; she had the unattractive habit of giving unsolicited advice to *everyone* she met. She told female cashiers at grocery stores what shade of lipstick they should wear, she pontificated to salespeople in the mall about how they could better serve customers, she gave advice to waitresses about how to do their job and to other service personnel she came upon. She analyzed pretty much every person who crossed her path. So you can imagine what she was like in her personal relationships. She was a "Karen."

In fact, Sarah's Fixer Imposter was so relentless that she basically made a mess of her personal relationships. People perceived her as controlling and holier-than-thou—no one more so than her own spouse. He got so fed up with her trying to "fix" him that he found solace in the arms of another woman. (News flash: people sometimes turn to adultery or polyamory to "fix" their relationships, which in turn creates new problems that need to be "fixed.")

"I can see problems in everyone else's lives," Sarah explained to me one day. "I'm empathic. But I have difficulty embracing my own issues. Please help me dig deeper. I have to get the pain out of me. It feels like a heavy weight."

I was impressed that Sarah had enough self-awareness to realize that behind her chronic advice-giving, she was harboring an emotional burden. It was time for some S.O.U.L. work.

I asked Sarah to get quiet and sit in front of me. It was time for her to STOP and get centered. I held her hands, and we engaged in a few moments of eye-gazing to get connected and focused. Finally I felt her drop into a quiet place. "I want you to do a little exercise that I call 'Name That Imposter,'" I told her.

She looked at me quizzically at first, then smiled. "OK, I'm game."

"What's holding you back?" I asked. "Self-esteem, self-loathing, fear, shame, guilt? What has the biggest weight here?"

"Shame and guilt are holding me back," she replied without missing a beat. "I feel shame about my biological family and guilt about having moved far away and cutting off contact."

After a moment of silence, I pulled my chair closer to her. "When was the first time you felt this way? What was happening?"

Sarah was quiet again. I could sense her beginning to OBSERVE herself and her past. "The first time was when I lied to a boyfriend. I was seventeen years old. I told him that I was an only child, that my mom passed away, and that my father was a diplomat and always traveling and impossible to meet. I was feeling insecure because he wanted to meet my family after we'd had sex and gotten more serious."

"Tell me more about your family—how they might have fostered shame in you."

"My mother is the root of my shame and fear. I grew up terrified that I'd turn into a pathological liar, just like her." Sarah's eyes welled up with tears. "She was an alcoholic who managed to lie her way through life—that is, when she wasn't drunk. I vowed never to be like her."

"What did being an alcoholic look like in your house?"

"My mom would pass out frequently. Sometimes she'd come home with lipstick smeared all over her face and pass out in the bathtub. She wasn't there for me and my siblings when we needed her. She was concerned with her own life, with men, and with numbing things out with booze. She couldn't feel. It hurt her too much. So not only did I never feel love or warmth from her—I became like *her* parent. I tried to keep things under control and fix her life. It was a huge burden."

I could feel that now, slowly but surely, Sarah was not only OBSERVING her past, but she was also starting to UNDERSTAND how it had coalesced into a Fixer Imposter.

"Instead of dealing with my own pain and confusion around my mother," Sarah continued, "I chose to work to avoid others. I also tried to help or fix people as a way to create order in other people's lives." Turns out that when Sarah made time for others in her life, she spent it pushing self-help books on them and trying to get them to unpack their issues so she could "fix" them, like a dime-store therapist.

Inevitably, Sarah fell under the weight of her Fixer Imposter. She got so overextended that her world collapsed. She alienated her kids and pushed away everyone who meant anything to her. She was sad, alone, riddled with anxiety, and broke. She had tried to be perfect—the antithesis of her mother. Since she grew up in chaos, she wanted extreme order. She worked all the time and figured she was doing something positive for her family by providing for them, but she was emotionally absent from them. Despite her good intentions, absent is absent. She couldn't communicate and really listen because she was too busy either shielding herself from pain or trying to control everything around her. As a result, her kids withdrew from her. Everyone in the family felt alone and empty inside.

Sarah eventually LIBERATED herself by OBSERVING and UNDERSTANDING how and why her Fixer Imposter had rooted itself in her psyche based on her upbringing. She took time to learn how to listen and be present for her family—in short, she recognized the value of having a life, not just making a living.

Life needs balance. Love and safety come in many forms: personal touch, quality time spent in nature and with friends and family, and so on. Every day Sarah spoke aloud the affirmations that we developed together about the life she wanted to create. She said those affirmations every day as if her life depended on it—and in a way, it did. When she messed up, she forgave herself and got back on track instead of punishing herself for not being perfect. And she incorporated many of the self-forgiveness exercises that you'll find in the last part of this book.

The Fixer Imposter can be your biggest superpower or your biggest foe. Because once you "fix" something—whether it's a concrete issue or an emotional state of mind (and let's face it: the list is endless)—often another fastball comes along that needs fixing again. That's pretty much the classic definition of a "vicious cycle." But if you practice the S.O.U.L. exercise on a regular basis, you'll keep the vicious cycles at bay.

What's often at play behind the motives of the Fixer Imposter is an unconscious desire to control things. And that's because people with dominant Fixer Imposters might have felt a lack of control growing up. That led to a controlling nature as an adult, or an unconscious tendency to direct and manage that can run amok. And trust me, it *can* run amok, because the world is imperfect and humans are flawed, so just about everything needs

> **S.O.U.L. is a powerful exercise that leads to a truly transformative way of looking at the world. Instead of seeing problems to fix, we see solutions to manifest. Instead of focusing on the "thing" to fix, we focus on the way we think about fixing it. In other words, we learn to understand the power of the mind. As author and publishing maverick Louise Hay put it, "I do not fix problems. I fix my thinking. Then problems fix themselves."**

to be "fixed."

Or does it?

At their best, Fixer Imposters are the world's healers and menders. They understand that the most effective application of their superpower is not so much in what they "fix," but in understanding what lies behind their impulse to want to do so. The S.O.U.L. exercise is a way to keep that in check.

S.O.U.L. is a powerful exercise that leads to a truly transformative way of looking at the world. Instead of seeing problems to fix, we see solutions to manifest. Instead of focusing on the "thing" to fix, we focus on the way we think about fixing it. In other words, we learn to understand the power of the mind. As author and publishing maverick Louise Hay put it, "I do not fix problems. I fix my thinking. Then problems fix themselves."

A QUICK RECAP OF THE FIXER IMPOSTER

People with this well-intentioned Imposter in the driver's seat are often preoccupied with "fixing" things—whether it's themselves or other people. But underneath this desire to make things "better" or "fix" something or someone, there is often a need to control things or exert dominance.

Under the guise of being helpful, people with dominant Fixer Imposters can be overbearing, overearnest, and overwhelming. And by always trying to "fix" things, they often end up giving away their own power.

The Superpower: *Solution-oriented, compassionate, giving*
The Saboteur: *Controlling, micromanaging, fear-driven*

THE
OVER
THINKER

CHAPTER 8

THE OVERTHINKER

We are dying from overthinking. We are slowly killing ourselves by thinking about everything. Think. Think. Think. You can never trust the human mind anyway. It's a death trap.

—Anthony Hopkins

There's a famous definition of insanity that says "doing the same thing over and over again and expecting different results." But here's another definition for you: going crazy is *thinking* about the same thing over and over again and expecting a different result, no matter how large or small that "thing" might be. The list of things to overthink goes on and on: *What should I do with my life? Should I quit my job and live on a goat farm in Mexico? Should I get an MBA and go into finance? What do I know about finance? Should I go on that keto diet? Did I blow it on that date last night? Did I talk too much? What did they mean when they said I seemed "funny"? Did they mean funny as in "ha-ha," or funny as in weird? Should I be practical or creative? Why can't I just be present in the moment? What is the moment, anyhow?*

Where is the "off" button?

Welcome to the world of the Overthinker Imposter, a master saboteur.

If you have a dominant Overthinker Imposter, you'll have a hard time finding that "off" button, because you'll be too busy overthinking why you overthink about things in the first place. With each successive "think it over again," new questions and thoughts emerge that lead to more overthinking. The result is paralysis by analysis, which inevitably leads to an emotional or mental gridlock that prevents you from moving forward in life. You not only overanalyze; you overmonitor, overevaluate, and ultimately try to control things with the sheer power of your mind.

There's a term for this tricky cycle: it's called a mental clusterfuck.

The Overthinker Imposter is a killjoy on so many levels. For starters, overthinking often creates procrastination, which inevitably leads to roadblocks. You overthink so much that you push things into the indefinite future. *I'll (over)think it later,* you say to yourself. The Overthinker Imposter also sucks the life out of spontaneity and positive risk-taking—both of which fuel change. If you have a dominant Overthinker Imposter in your driver's seat, you rarely get out of your comfort zone, where meaningful personal growth happens, because you're too busy manufacturing questions in your head. But by keeping your discomfort zone at bay, you also keep at bay experiences that can enhance your creative, emotional, or professional mojo. Then you wonder why life feels so empty. And you overthink *that.*

Metaphorically, this is like hovering at the edge of a diving board, contemplating the water at the deep end: *Will it be too cold? Will I belly flop? Will my swimsuit come off? Is the water deep enough?* Of course, if you take this metaphor to the extreme, you never jump off that board into the water. You stand at the edge, overthinking what will happen if you do. And so life passes you by. Other people nudge you aside, dive in, and swim away. Meanwhile you stand there unable to leap, even if a net is right in front of you. And even if you *do* eventually leap, you often undermine your experience by questioning it with what you should have, could have, or would have done differently. (Yep, the "shoulda, woulda, coulda" problem.)

THE SUPERPOWERS OF THE OVERTHINKER IMPOSTER

The Overthinker Imposter shares a common border with the Fixer Imposter, as I mentioned in our previous chapter, insofar as it is a master worrier and obsessively asks, "What if?" This leads to indecision and ambivalence, which is not always a bad thing. There's also a positive aspect to this. The superpower of this Imposter is being able to see multiple sides of an issue and different points of view. That is a powerful gift when you're faced with truly complex issues that need to be carefully considered from all angles. People with a dominant Overthinker Imposter are often ethical, reliable, idealistic, honest, and detail-oriented.

Here's another silver lining to this Imposter: overthinking goes hand in glove with ambivalence, which is sometimes considered a sign of intelligence, since multiple truths and moral realities can and often *do* coexist. Author F. Scott Fitzgerald once wrote, "The test of a first-rate intelligence is the ability to hold two opposed ideas in the mind at the same time, and still retain the ability to function."[5] If you're driven by a dominant Overthinker Imposter, you can probably hold not just two but three or four opposed ideas in mind at the same time. That is a blessing but can also become a curse if it ends up hindering your "ability to function." And guess what? It often does.

Overthinking is a process we share as human beings, of course, and it starts early in life: "What do I want to be when I grow up?" That's an essential question you've no doubt asked yourself at one point or another. If your answer to that question was "I have no idea," well, you're not alone. Some people come into the world knowing exactly what their passion and purpose is in life. Yo-Yo Ma was probably playing cello in the womb.

But most people don't know what they want to be when they grow up—or who they are. They have passions and interests. It's

5. F. Scott Fitzgerald, "The Crack-Up," *Esquire*, 1936, https://www.esquire.com/lifestyle/a4310/the-crack-up/.

normal to think about them, but infinitely better to *explore* them. People with dominant Overthinker Imposters have a hard time doing the latter because they obsessively second-guess themselves. (News flash: second-guessing and overthinking usually go together.) And so instead of drilling down into their Authentic Selves to find out who they really are (their true purpose) and what's behind their overthinking, they become procrastinators par excellence. Or, on the flip side of that, they try every new thing in the book: One day they're going to be a writer. The next day they think maybe they're better suited to be a pilot. Or a stockbroker. Or maybe a teacher. Hey, what about real estate?

We all make many important decisions every day, from what to eat and where to live to whom we marry. But if we're driven by an Overthinker Imposter, we overthink almost *every* decision, large or small. I've witnessed firsthand how the Overthinker Imposter can stifle people because they can't turn the "shoulda, woulda, coulda" tape off in their heads. Overthinking isn't about reflecting and meditating on stressful situations, which can help you confront difficult issues and solve personal problems. Rather, it's more like perpetual worrying: a process that hinders your resolve and your ability to act, resulting in indecision, fear, and negativity.

Some people with dominant Overthinker Imposters feel compelled to convince people that they're "smart," "interesting," or "intelligent," usually because they're worried that they might seem stupid, uninteresting, or unintelligent. They judge themselves so severely that out of insecurity, they try to project an image that others will validate. If that sounds like you, then you probably have an Overthinker Imposter *and* a Judge Imposter duking it out in your head. (See the next chapter for more about the Judge Imposter.)

THE S.O.U.L. OF THE OVERTHINKER IMPOSTER

Tara was one such person with a dominant Overthinker Imposter. She was the daughter of a longtime client. She seemingly had it all. Athletic and gorgeous, she was at the top of her high school class with a 4.8 average. "Her future is so bright," her mom used to say, "that everyone has to wear shades around her."

But guess what? Tara didn't share that perspective. In fact, she was absolutely terrified of the future. Her brain wouldn't shut down. She constantly stressed about making a wrong decision, from whether to eat toast or a muffin for breakfast to where to go to college. Her family tried to give her advice, but it was drowned out by all the conflicting voices in her head.

"My mom tells me that if I don't go to college, I'll regret it for the rest of my life," Tara told me when we were still getting to know one another. "But I have to pay my own way. My dad went to college, but he's regretted that decision his whole life. He thinks he should have worked his way up the corporate ladder instead of getting into the medical field."

I listened patiently. For someone so young, Tara certainly had a lot on her mind.

"My uncle offered me a job working for him in construction, which I really like. It pays good money. He told me that college won't get me anywhere in this economy except in debt. I just don't know what to think!"

As I do with all my clients, I asked Tara to STOP. It was time for her to get centered and quiet the ruckus of voices in her head. I did a brief guided meditation with Tara. Open-minded and bighearted, she dropped right into it, closing her eyes and breathing deeply. After ten minutes I gave her a piece of paper and a wild-writing exercise. Sometimes called freewriting, this process cuts through the critical mind. Using a writing prompt, you keep your pen on your paper and write totally uncensored

and nonstop, not trying to be clever or impress anyone, jotting down whatever comes to mind. Tara's writing prompt was this:
"I am a person who . . ."

The benefits of meditation calm the mind, body, and soul the same way that being silent does. The act of practicing silence helps lower blood pressure and boosts the body's immune system and brain chemistry. And it creates space for us to hear— and ultimately calm—the chatter in our brains. We become more aligned with our intuition and more in touch with our emotions. We're more centered and anchored to the calm center within. The ultimate benefit? When life gets stormy, we can live in the eye of that storm rather than get tossed about in its headwinds.

Tara wrote nonstop using that prompt. She didn't think about what her parents, uncles and aunts, and siblings might say. She wrote about her dreams and her interests, which ran the gamut from being an engineer to a construction worker to a fashion designer. Then I gave her another fifteen minutes to complete the "Mind Dump," a SoulBlazing exercise in which she wrote down as many positives and negatives as she could think of for each of her choices. Visualizing the pros and cons of any situation puts the Overthinker Imposter in the back seat; it shifts your focus instead to the words on the page.

After these writing exercises, I guided Tara through a series of meditations. In the course of these exercises, Tara was able to OBSERVE her tendency to let other people's voices into her head—so much so that she would overthink and second-guess her own desires and inclinations. She was able to step outside herself and comprehend how her "monkey mind" fueled her Overthinker Imposter. "Monkey mind" is a Buddhist term for the constant chatter and negative self-talk that goes on in our heads. Because the mind is so frenetic, it can obsessively flit from one thing to another like (you guessed it) monkeys on a vine. The only way to quiet the mind and stop all that mental monkey madness is through meditation and silence. There are more meditation apps on your cell phone than there are monkeys in the jungle, so there's no excuse for not starting a meditation practice.

The benefits of meditation calm the mind, body, and soul the same way that being silent does. The act of practicing silence helps lower blood pressure and boosts the body's immune system and brain chemistry. And it creates space for us to hear—and ultimately calm—the chatter in our brains. We become more aligned with our intuition and more in touch with our emotions. We're more centered and anchored to the calm center within. The ultimate benefit? When life gets stormy, we can live in the eye of that storm rather than get tossed about in its headwinds. We're able to respond gently to life instead of reacting irrationally to it.

Yes, meditating and practicing silence can do all that, and here's the good news when it came to Tara: she was young. It's incredibly empowering to learn these practices before your self-limiting beliefs grow so rigid that you have to drill down into them like asphalt. Tara was able to not only apply meditation techniques to quiet her mind but also UNDERSTAND the importance of having a ritual that silenced the Overthinker Imposter. Once she reached those still inner waters, she could get clarity on what was true and meaningful for *her*—not for her mother, her father, or anyone outside herself. That helped her not become overwhelmed by the responsibility of making big decisions in life. This, in turn, LIBERATED her from the constant push-pull of other people's voices in her head. It also helped her UNDERSTAND that you don't have to decide *everything* immediately, especially when you tend to overthink things. Life is a process and a work in progress.

After our sessions, during which she fine-tuned her ability to focus in the present on her true core values, Tara sent out her college applications and got offers from diverse colleges. One even offered her a full ride for a degree in engineering. It was a no-brainer for Tara; she decided that she would follow that path. In fact, Tara didn't really make the decision; instead, the decision came to her. By knowing her strengths, desires, and goals (and writing them down, thereby making them *real*), the answers emerged. They were in her all along, and yet it seemed as if she let them come to her.

The Overthinker Imposter is multifaceted: People with this Imposter in the driver's seat usually have sharp intellects and the ability to see the world from many different perspectives. But they can easily tumble down the rabbit hole of worry, constant second-guessing, and chronic indecision. You can procrastinate away your life by overthinking because you never fully commit or dive fully out of your comfort zone.

I know plenty of people, both personally and professionally, who lived their whole lives with unrealized dreams because their Overthinker Imposters were so dominant. One of my closest friends always wanted to tell her life story in a book—it was hugely important to her. But her Overthinker Imposter was constantly in the way, telling her that she didn't have the writing chops, warning her that other people would weigh in on her prose and judge her, perpetuating her writer's block until she had paralysis by analysis. She passed away without writing that book, and a thousand stories were left unwritten. Many of my clients with Overthinker Imposters give up on or procrastinate away their dreams like my friend did. I always think of author Maya Angelou, who wrote, "There is no greater agony than bearing an untold story inside you" (*I Know Why the Caged Bird Sings*, 1969).

Once you're able to understand and quiet your Overthinker Imposter and release the insecurities that fuel its mental chatter, you can move forward in life with an eye on your true North Star.

A QUICK RECAP OF THE OVERTHINKER IMPOSTER

People with dominant Overthinker Imposters often have a hard time finding the "off" button because they're too busy overthinking. With each successive thought, new questions and reflections emerge that lead to more overthinking. The result is paralysis by analysis, which inevitably leads to an emotional or mental gridlock that prevents forward momentum in life. They not only overanalyze; they overmonitor, overevaluate, and ultimately try to control things with the sheer power of their minds.

The Superpower: *The ability to see multiple points of view, detail-oriented, reliable*
The Saboteur: *Procrastination, second-guessing, indecision*

THE JUDGE

CHAPTER 9

THE JUDGE

Judging a person does not define who they are; it defines who you are.

—Source unknown

A re you judgmental of yourself and others? I mean *really* judgmental? Do you find fault with just about everyone (including yourself) and everything, from the sublime to the ridiculous? Are you maybe a teeny-tiny wee bit snobbish? Or do you just find that you can add an "un" to adjectives that describe most people (as in *uninteresting, uncool, unappealing, unaware,* and *unimportant*)? If that's you or someone you know, chances are high the Judge Imposter is at the helm.

The Judge archetype is connected to justice and judgment. Without justice, bad people run amok and get away with bad shit. And without judgment—that is, without a judge to assess a situation in order to administer the law—there is no justice.

Ergo, the judge is the ultimate icon of wisdom and authority in society. They are the supreme leaders and arbiters of honesty, due process, and morality. That's a big load to carry. No wonder the symbol of Lady Justice comes with so many accessories. You know who I'm talking about: she's the allegorical representation of justice we see in courts of law who's depicted blindfolded, holding scales and a sword. The scales represent the weighing of evidence in a situation with respect to the law. The sword represents authority, which can quickly and decisively slice through bullshit to determine what's true or false, and who's innocent or guilty. And the blindfold? Well, the blindfold signifies impartiality: in theory the judge makes an assessment without regard to race, gender, economic status, or looks.

People with dominant Judge Imposters who aren't self-aware or mature use personal biases and high standards against others—and often (here's the real rub) against themselves. And since in our society judges have the final say on matters, determining what's right or wrong according to the law, people with dominant Judge Imposters always think that *they're* right. There's usually no convincing these judgmental individuals that there might be a different way to assess things. It's their way or the proverbial highway. When these people are narcissists in positions of political power—and they also have uncontrollable Egotist Imposters—they often become dangerous tyrants who judge people according to race, skin color, gender, or religion. I won't name names, but our history books and TV news are filled with autocrat bullies who've wreaked havoc in society and the world at large.

You might have guessed by now that the Judge Imposter shares a bed with the Overthinker Imposter and the Fixer Imposter, insofar as they view the world with a critical eye: people with dominant Judge Imposters assess everything and everyone, sometimes with painstaking severity. But when they turn that judgment on themselves, the low self-esteem and negative self-talk can go off the charts: I'm not good enough, cool enough, rich enough, smart enough, pretty enough—fill in the blank. That negative self-talk can go on and on. With the dominant Judge Imposter, you probably cast your critical eye on what people do for a living, what they wear, what car they drive, who their friends are, what their house looks like, what neighborhood they live in, and so on.

The Judge Imposter can be so harsh that it squeezes the life out of just about every experience. Moments of joy and freedom vaporize. It's emotionally debilitating. If your Judge Imposter is in the driver's seat, you probably tend to forget your heart in favor of your mind. The rational and dispassionate virtue of an impartial judge can become irrational and cold, which is the shadow side of the Judge archetype. You might even have a tendency to be a bit holier-than-thou, even though under all that hubris there's usually an insecure inner child whose judgmental nature is hiding a lot of self-doubt.

Yep, that inner child—it just doesn't go away, does it?

THE SUPERPOWERS OF THE JUDGE IMPOSTER

The Judge Imposter, however, is also a formidable superpower because our lives depend in many ways on the cool-headed objectivity that informs this Imposter. Think about it: without the virtues of justice, our modern society would look like a cross between *Lord of the Flies* and *Tiger King*. And that's why, on the positive side, people with dominant Judge Imposters are often levelheaded, even-tempered individuals with an uncanny ability to stay centered. In relationships they're the good listeners with a shoulder you can lean on. They have a sense of right and wrong, and a tendency to ignore personal biases in the interest of upholding high standards.

Everyone could use a doctor, a lawyer, and a person with a positive dominant Judge Imposter!

THE S.O.U.L. OF THE JUDGE IMPOSTER

I've seen my fair share of clients with dominant Judge Imposters. Many of them are brilliant and creative individuals, with strong intellects and a philosophical bent. And where I live in Los Angeles, many of them enjoy the Hollywood spotlight and are prima donnas par excellence. George, a successful composer, was a perfect example.

George will gladly tell you and everyone he comes across that he's a famous composer. And he was, indeed, quite a talented man, scoring a dozen films in the 1980s and 1990s, some highly successful. His name was known even in casual Hollywood circles, and he loved the glitz and glamour that went with that badge.

The problem was that any time George worked with a director on a soundtrack, his arrogance and Judge Imposter got in the way. He imposed his views and judgments on every musical score, regardless of how others involved in the same project weighed in on it. And of course, he was always "right." Instead of listening to the director who had artistic control over the film and called the shots (literally and figuratively), George went down with his intellectual guns blazing and his Judge Imposter in full combat gear.

"I've lived all over the world. I've made love to beautiful women. I've scored the most famous films in a dozen countries. What have *you* done?" was apparently one of his favorite lines to use on directors. He judged them as "the entitled kids who graduated from USC with a piece of paper that tells them they know how to create art." His Judge Imposter didn't give any latitude for these people to contradict or exist outside his own predetermined judgments about them.

You probably know where this story is going to end: George's Judge Imposter was so relentless that he was fired repeatedly from high-profile projects. Word spread and his reputation was tarnished. Eventually, he went from an in-demand millionaire with a candy-apple red Ferrari in the driveway of his Hollywood Hills mansion to a litigant in a bank foreclosure. That's when he ended up on my couch.

"I'm self-taught," he said the first day I worked with him. A self-made man, he endured a difficult childhood in eastern Europe, mastered music at a young age, and never stopped learning. He didn't waste a minute of his life (as long as he was writing music, that is), and he retained everything he had ever heard or read. And he thought that everyone else should be exactly the same way.

To his credit, deep down George was sweet, spiritual, and intellectual. He'd been exposed to different world cultures and was open to the unique experiences of each one. Even the people who fired him from various projects never questioned his dedication to the task. But there was something over-the-top about his Judge Imposter and the way he clung to the past, nostalgically waxing poetic about every past job and every missed opportunity—and judging *other* people who couldn't meet his high standards.

And so early on in our work together, I cut to the chase with George. He was talking about the last film he'd scored and judging everyone who had been on the team. He was not only stuck in the past; he had also created a smoke screen for himself to mask the pain of not being the top dog.

"George," I said, trying to get him back in his body. It took me a few seconds to break him out of the trance he'd talked himself into. "Listen, we're putting you on a no-judgment diet. For our next several sessions together, I'd like you to refrain from talking about *any* famous people you know, *any* movies you scored, or *anything* involving your knowledge, thoughts, or judgments about the entertainment industry. *Nothing!*" I was asking George to put his Judge Imposter aside and STOP in his tracks.

I then took him through a fifteen-minute meditation. George's strong mind helped him focus. After the meditation we held hands and looked into each other's eyes in silence for three minutes of eye-gazing.

When I finally felt George get quiet inside and relax his critical mind, I leaned forward. "I want you to share with me what is going on in your mind—*without words*, George."

He stared into my eyes. I saw the change come over him within a couple of minutes. First there was silence. Then connection. Thoughts and feelings in *real time*.

He exhaled and shut his eyes for a few minutes while I held space for him. Finally he said, "What a feeling not to be 'on' and to feel accepted."

I smiled.

"I'm getting that I'm not my career, my past, or my future. I need to hang on to this feeling because I feel OK. I like me just as I am." All of a sudden, George began to cry. "You know," he began, "my parents were crazy high achievers. They were both concert pianists in Budapest who ended up performing in the country's top concert halls. There was never a possibility that I wouldn't follow in their footsteps. But not only that . . ."

George sighed and tried to hold back more tears. He was in the process of OBSERVING the forces that had shaped his Judge Imposter: well-intentioned but overbearing parents who projected their own ambitions onto George. "Not only that," he continued, "but I was expected to do better than them. How could I possibly do better than parents who performed in the equivalent of Carnegie Hall?"

Through the course of our work, with a mix of meditation and reflection, George began to UNDERSTAND how important it was to free himself from the pressure he had put on himself his whole life. He had never felt like he was good enough or that he could ever reach the high bar that his parents had set. Eventually, he was able to comprehend why he felt like such a failure by constantly comparing his present life to his past glories.

It was a watershed moment. George realized who he could be without the Judge Imposter weighing him down. And that was the beginning of George's LIBERATION.

Soon after our work together, George went on a pilgrimage to Machu Picchu. He wanted to look at life with the big picture in mind and think about his legacy beyond just music. Far away from the pressures of his familiar world, in the magical environment of Peru, George decided to say goodbye to his old life and change tracks completely. He decided to leave the music industry altogether and reinvent himself by diving into a passion he never thought he could pursue for a living.

George had always loved interior design—he collected antiques his whole life and had a house filled with paintings and unique objects from around the world. Upon his return to the States, George found a job at a boutique antique furniture store, where he flourished. A year later he got an offer to score music for another movie, but despite the decent wage, he declined and attended workshops in curation, art history, and interior design.

George basically reinvented himself. And he was able to do that only by wrangling with his Judge Imposter. But doing so isn't easy in a world where advertising feeds on our insecurities, fueling our most judgmental tendencies. Having lived a long time in Los Angeles with its cult of "beautiful people," I know this firsthand. If your Judge Imposter obscures your ability to see beyond surface glam, you never experience people for who they *really* are. I've also traveled enough to know two things about beauty: (1) it is truly in the eye of the beholder (along with the judgments in the beholder's mind), and (2) it is informed by the culture you grew up in: what's judged as beautiful in one culture might be bland or uninteresting in another.

For example, I encountered the most weather-beaten, dust-laden, tooth-deprived, hair-matted nomad you could possibly imagine in the desert of Petra. And you know what? He was absolutely beautiful, both inside and out. He was full of natural self-esteem that was endorsed by his culture, where the kind of made-up glam we have in Western culture isn't valued. Judgments, in other words, are relative.

When I modeled in Tokyo, I worked with many people who had dominant Judge Imposters. Their worldview revolved around status: hanging out with the "movers and shakers" who had lots of money and power. That said, one of my best friends was an extraordinary, humble fifty-two-year-old taxi driver named Yoshio. We met in his cab, and after several weeks he asked me to teach him English. For the next few months, we met twice a week for two hours each session. We shared everything with each other. I told him about my crazy life while working in Japan and the different people I came into contact with, and he shared stories about his brothers, sisters, friends, and boss. He was an authentic, real person who became my best friend in Japan.

> **When the Judge Imposter is our superpower, we're able to see the world with clarity and impartiality. But when this Imposter works against us, it feeds our judgmental nature and we become our own worst critic.**

I got an inside look into the part of Japanese culture that was simple—the local diners, the slow trains, the hole-in-the-wall mom-and-pop shops—and I met salt-of-the-earth people. It was very different from the side of Japan I had come to know—the hottest clubs with thousand-dollar entry fees and hidden VIP rooms that looked like small apartments, as well as trips to upscale hot springs and old cities.

I learned more from my friendship with Yoshio than I ever learned from any designer, model, or millionaire because he taught me about the importance of *simplicity* in life. Had I allowed my Judge Imposter to get in the way, I would have dismissed him from the get-go and robbed myself of the richness of our friendship. Twenty years later, he's still one of my close friends.

The Judge is a powerful force not only in our society at large but also in our entertainment culture. We adore shows like *American Idol* and *Dancing with the Stars* in which experts judge the contestants. We love the tension of watching people win and lose under the keen eye of these expert judges. Hey, we even love the stern Judge Judy, who is so no-bullshit that she once famously said to someone on the witness stand, "Sir, don't pee on my leg and tell me that it's raining" (*Don't Pee on My Leg and Tell Me It's Raining*, 1997).

When the Judge Imposter is our superpower, we're able to see the world with clarity and impartiality. But when this Imposter works against us, it feeds our judgmental nature and we become our own worst critic. Integrating the Judge Imposter is a noble act that comes through self-awareness and the ongoing practice of truth-telling.

A QUICK RECAP OF THE JUDGE IMPOSTER

People with dominant Judge Imposters are judgmental of themselves and the world at large. If they don't get a grip on this dominant Imposter, it can inhibit them, making them bitter critics. Growing in self-awareness and telling the truth are necessary for integrating this Imposter.

The Superpower: *Wise, honest, impartial*
The Saboteur: *Critical, domineering, close-minded*

PART THREE

Tools and Exercises

CHAPTER 10

UNPACKING OUR EMOTIONAL BAGGAGE

*When the deepest part of you
becomes engaged in what you are
doing, when your activities and
actions become gratifying and
purposeful, when what you do
serves both yourself and others,
when you do not tire within but
seek the sweet satisfaction of your
life and your work, you are doing
what you were meant to be doing.*

—Gary Zukav, *The Seat of the Soul*, 2014

D ear readers, I'm sorry to keep hitting you over the head with this frying pan, but it bears repeating: our Imposters might manifest themselves in our personalities in different ways, but they all come from the same place. They're all rooted in our childhoods. No one gets out of childhood unscathed, even those of you who may have had a seemingly perfect childhood. (News flash: there's no such thing.) The majority of us human beings have experienced some form of emotional distress in our formative years, including bona fide abuse.

That abuse can come in obvious forms or in more subjective emotional forms. Maybe we were neglected or overprotected. Or we were raised by unconscious parents who inflicted their own unresolved issues on us. I'm going to bet that most of us had parents who had emotional work to do on themselves that was left unattended and thus transferred onto us.

Whatever the case may be, we all need to do spiritual and emotional housecleaning, and these exercises are part of that process. They're designed to help you become aware of your own unconscious beliefs and patterns. Those beliefs and patterns may have served us well when we were kids. But now that we're all grown up, they simply don't work. Imagine wearing clothes designed for your eight-year-old body when, in fact, you're twenty-eight. Or thirty-eight. Or fifty-eight. The experience is constraining at best and painful at worst.

You can do some of these exercises once and others on a regular basis. Either way, they will serve you your entire life.

1. *Inventory of Hurts*
2. *Grieve Your Pain*
3. *Write a Blame Letter*
4. *Write Your Own Eulogy*
5. *Solo Striptease*
6. *Into the Looking Glass*
7. *Selflessness Boot Camp*
8. *The Shame Game*
9. *Your Visionary Mission*
10. *Return to Wonder*
11. *Claim Your Morning*

EXERCISE 1: INVENTORY OF HURTS

MANY OF US ARE LIKE chipmunks, packing away our hurt feelings and bruised egos like little nuts, holding on to them for dear life and identifying with them even if they don't serve us. And guess what? They rarely do.

Some of those wounds and hurts might be colossal. They might have been a systemic and regular form of physical or emotional abuse. Or they might have been less obvious. For example, perhaps you had a parent who always lowered the bar for you because they didn't think you could rise to an occasion—thus silently communicating that you weren't up to par in some fundamental way. You believed that you were stupid when, in fact, you were not. But you logged that into your emotional storehouse, and it became part of your emotional inventory—your inventory of hurts.

This exercise is designed to unpack the source of emotional wounds that still define you to one degree or another and trip you up in life. By bringing them to light—by identifying them, looking at them, examining them from the vantage point of time, and giving them a voice—you're able to reframe them. You can disown them and release them. But first, you have to face them.

Here are the steps:

- SIT DOWN AND MAKE A list of all the hurts and wounds you've experienced. Free your mind and don't censor yourself. Write them all down. Be specific: What exactly happened? What words were exchanged? When? Where were you? How did you feel?

- NAME NAMES. IT'S OK IN this exercise to point fingers at the people who might have been involved

This exercise is designed to unpack the source of emotional wounds that still define you to one degree or another and trip you up in life. By bringing them to light—by identifying them, looking at them, examining them from the vantage point of time, and giving them a voice— you're able to reframe them. You can disown them and release them. But first, you have to face them.

in your distress. Give them a voice so that you can ultimately forgive them (and yourself) and release them.

- READ THEM OVER. HOW DO you feel? Allow yourself to experience whatever emotion comes up, but remind yourself that the experience does not define you, particularly if it happened long ago.
- VERBALLY REFRAME AND REVERSE WHATEVER emotion rooted itself in your heart and soul at that time. If you felt stupid, tell yourself that you are smart. If you were told that you're ugly, tell yourself that you are beautiful. Disown the perception and the experience. And yes, I know that's easier said than done. Some of the later exercises go into more depth on how to go from self-loathing to self-love.

- BURN YOUR LIST. YES, GO for it. Take the list and light it on fire. Like the Burning Man effigy at the Burning Man festival, leave no trace. Purging things in fire is a healing ritual from the ancients that you can incorporate into your life today.
- RETURN THE "GIFT." You don't need to accept every gift given to you. It's your choice. Imagine telling the giver "No, thank you."

This Buddhist parable can help us offset lingering hurts in our emotional inventories. It goes like this: Imagine that someone gave you a gift—but it's a toxic gift. They spent a lot of time and energy wrapping it. They bought it and wrapped it *specifically* for you. But when they offer you the gift, you don't accept it. Despite the gift-giver's prodding, you don't yield.

By not accepting the "gift," you release it back to the giver. You don't own it. It does not belong to you. It does not define you. It now belongs back in the hands of the person who's giving.

Now imagine that the "gift" was actually something painful: a deeply hurtful comment that lodged in your heart. An insult or harsh judgment directed at you by someone, one that was so deeply wounding that *you* allowed it to define you in some way, *even though it was more a reflection of the other person.*

Let's repeat that: we're talking about negative or toxic input directed at you by someone *that you allowed to define you in some way, even though it was a reflection of the other person—not you.*

Remember: the gift does not belong to you or define you. Imagine what your life would look like if you never accepted it in the first place.

The Inventory of Hurts exercise is a way of describing the "gifts" that wounded you. Return each "gift." Disown them. They were likely never yours to begin with. Rather, they belonged to the sender.

EXERCISE 2: GRIEVE YOUR PAIN

QUEEN ELIZABETH II ONCE SAID that grief is "the price we pay for love." I would add that it's also the price we pay for loss. And even if we are losing emotional pain that has somehow come to define us, there is grief: the grief that comes from the attachment to something that has been part of our lives for so long.

Here's the exercise: if the previous exercise stirs up grief, you need to let it out. You might need to take a hike into nature and scream into a canyon, or go into your bedroom and beat up your pillow. Or you might simply want to just sit in your favorite spot in nature and cry—*really* cry—from your gut. No holding back. No censoring.

If you find it difficult to summon these powerful emotions, listen to sad music that stirs your soul or watch a few sad movies that really move you. Open up to your own sadness. It's only in allowing yourself to really acknowledge and feel emotions that you're able to let them go. This might sound simple, and it is, but that doesn't mean it's easy. Giving yourself permission to really grieve is difficult in our fast-paced world, where you're supposed to "move on" as quickly as possible.

But our inner worlds don't operate according to the clock. Allowing ourselves to experience and express grief is such a fundamental part of healing that Dr. Siddhartha Mukherjee considers it part of his medical arsenal. "Grieving is a natural part of medicine," he writes. "If you deny that, again, you'd get in this trap of curing and victory."

Curing is not healing. And victory is not release.

EXERCISE 3: WRITE A BLAME LETTER

OK, so usually we'd tell you that blame is not a great thing. Blame is the act of assigning responsibility to someone or something else for a negative action that befell us. That someone might be *yourself*, by the way. Some of us are masters at blaming ourselves for everything and beating ourselves up ad nauseam. That's a surefire way of staying in victim mode most of our lives. On the other side of the spectrum, some of us blame *others* all the time. Everything is always someone else's fault. By some cosmic fluke, we are just never, ever responsible for our own shit. (Say hello to the Egotist Imposter.)

Both ways of being are toxic when they become pathological: Blaming others falsely empowers us. Blaming ourselves disempowers us.

But . . .

In this exercise, we're flipping blame on its head. We're giving you carte blanche to knock yourself out, blame away, and say "fuck you" to all the people you do implicate in negative or shitty experiences in life that went so deep that they informed you. Consider this a one-off: an opportunity to scream at the top of your lungs and express your anger at someone (or at many people, as is often the case) who pissed you off.

By identifying the people who hurt you (even if you had a hand at allowing that hurt to fester), you release a lot of emotional charge. This exercise is a fraternal twin to the Grieve Your Pain exercise. Here's how to go about it:

- Set a timer for five minutes, and write a letter to someone who did something negative or wounding in the past. Be specific. Start your letter with "[insert name], I blame you for [fill in the blank]."

- LET YOURSELF BE AS VINDICTIVE and angry as you want—no holds barred. Don't censor yourself. Keep writing until the timer goes off.
- REPEAT AND WRITE ANOTHER BLAME letter to anyone else who has hurt or wounded you in ways that still resonate in your soul.
- WHEN YOU'RE DONE, READ EACH letter out loud to yourself. There might be many people in your life whom you blame for various hurts. Include everyone. Take your time. *Listen closely to what your wounded inner child so desperately needs someone to recognize.*
- NOW TURN IT AROUND WITH some blame-shifting: Replace the name of the person who wronged you with *your* name, and reread each letter. Pay attention to how this makes you feel. When you flip this exercise around, you suddenly see how you, too, might have been complicit in wronging someone. Maybe you stole from someone. Or said something deeply hurtful. Or worse. We're all flawed. This exercise is an equal-opportunity employer of blame.

EXERCISE 4: WRITE YOUR OWN EULOGY

WE ALL KNOW THE SAYING that few people on their deathbed wish they'd spent more time in the office. No—when it's time to meet their maker, most people wish that they'd lived a fuller life: taken more emotional risks, tried harder to reach certain goals, expressed love more generously and spontaneously. They take stock of their passions and purpose, longing for more time to experience both.

That's why I'm a big believer in the practice of writing your own eulogy: it might sound creepy to you, but writing your own eulogy obliges you to take stock of your life so that, ideally, you align it with your passions and purpose *now*—while you're still alive on this beautiful planet we call Earth.

Most of us have heard a eulogy. It's a speech about someone who has died, often told in an inspirational fashion that focuses on the positive aspects of that person's life. It's the big-picture view of a person's trajectory through time, summing up their milestones.

Writing your own eulogy obliges you to take stock of your life so that, ideally, you align it with your passions and purpose *now*—while you're still alive on this beautiful planet we call Earth.

In this exercise, *you* are the subject of the eulogy. The focus is on yourself, looking back on your life. By default, this obliges you to envision experiences that you *haven't realized yet*. In his productivity classic *The 7 Habits of Highly Effective People* (2014), Stephen R. Covey asks us to "begin with the end in mind" and dedicates the second of his famous habits to this practice. According to Covey, Habit 2 is based on "the ability to envision in your mind what you cannot at present see with your eyes." Visualizing how you want to live your life sows the seeds of its manifestation. "If you don't make a conscious effort to visualize who you are and what you want in life," Covey writes, "then you empower other people and circumstances to shape you and your life by default."

Write your eulogy so that it reflects the life you *want* to lead, not the life that you haven't led yet because people or circumstances have, in theory, gotten in your way. I write "in theory" because we often blame others for what we haven't been able to achieve, when in reality our own Imposters get in our way, consciously or unconsciously.

This practice has the added benefit of cultivating an awareness of how you'll measure your life, or your legacy. When you measure your life against the success you've had in your career, you're often left feeling empty. But when you measure it against the values that feed your Authentic Soul, you're left with a meaningful legacy that brings huge emotional gratification. As someone once said, "it's not the years in your life that count; it's the life in your years."

So don't let your Imposters steal your life by turning you into a workaholic who pours all their energy into their job because they're afraid to love. Use your emotional intelligence to become aware of your Imposters so that the measure of your life is, indeed, the life in your years.

Circling back to our exercise, here's an easy template for writing your own eulogy:

- INTRODUCTION: Begin with a brief, personalized, heartfelt autobiographical opener that gives us a sense of who you were and what was important to you. Tell us where you were born and grew up, what your passions were, what you did for a living, and who the special people in your life were.
- TAKE IT FURTHER: Then try to articulate experiences in your life that taught you how to love, laugh, and live—simple lessons that have served you better than a library's worth of books. What are the three favorite stories from your life that exemplify those moments?
- GO DEEPER: Dig deep and honor yourself for the positive things you've achieved and experienced in life. Write about how you touched other people's lives, what you want your life to mean to them, and your dreams for others: friends, family, partners.

If you find this exercise hard to do—if you're stuck in a negative place and can't conjure up anything positive in your life—don't fret and don't put any pressure on yourself. There is no right or wrong way to write your eulogy. The point is to look back on your life as if you were standing at a vantage point, looking out over a sweeping landscape. What do you *want* to see? How do you *want* to have lived? What are the positive traits in yourself that you know reside deep down in your heart?

EXERCISE 5: SOLO STRIPTEASE

BEFORE YOU GET TOO EXCITED here, relax: this is an exercise between you and the mirror (no pole required). You're going to have to strip—literally—but you're taking it off for yourself. And what you're peeling away is not so much your jeans, but your negative self-talk about your body. You know what I'm talking about: *I'm too fat. I'm too skinny. I'm unattractive. I look like fill-in-the-blank.*

Ever since that first insult in the schoolyard, most of us have been internalizing criticism from other people or have been comparing ourselves to others or to the onslaught of "perfect people" we see in advertising. Sadly, some of us grew up with judgmental parents or siblings who threw a few daggers at us. Those stabs went deep and created body shame that we have lugged around our entire lives.

Body shame feeds on itself: it cultivates self-consciousness and inhibitions, which form a major barrier against expression of all kinds, from sexual to creative. We end up focusing on what our bodies *look* like rather than how they *feel*.

This exercise is designed to slowly dismantle body shame. It's so simple yet so incredibly difficult because it goes right to the heart of our self-loathing. It forces us to literally look at ourselves, then grapple with what comes up emotionally.

Are you ready?

- PLACE A CHAIR IN FRONT of a mirror, undress, sit down, and observe your body with a loving gaze. If that feels monumental, try to look at your body from a neutral place. Be aware of the judgments that crop up in your mind.

- NOTICE ALL ASPECTS OF YOUR body with an artist's appreciative eye, paying attention to each shape, line, and contour without passing judgment, either positive or negative. Did I say this was easy? No. I said it was simple. But that doesn't mean it's not going to provoke all sorts of discomfort. Well, guess what? You're going to have to sit with your discomfort. Because discomfort is where the juice is. There's no hall pass out of this one.

This exercise is designed to slowly dismantle body shame. It's so simple yet so incredibly difficult because it goes right to the heart of our self-loathing. It forces us to literally look at ourselves, then grapple with what comes up emotionally.

As you look at yourself, repeat the following affirmations:

My body is a gift from nature and the Universe.

Beauty is a state of mind, not a state of body.
Flaws are transformed by love and acceptance.

My body possesses power. It has its own wisdom, and I trust that wisdom completely.

*I choose to see the divine perfection in every cell of
my body.*

Take it a step further and tell yourself how much you love
those things you're trying not to hate on: *I love my double chin. I
love my knock-knees. I love my inner-tube belly!* I know, it sounds
impossible—even theatrical. But eventually the voice that says
"I'm unlovable" will diminish. You will remember that your body
serves you every day. It's OK to be different. Perfection is in the
eye of the beholder. As author Louise Hay wrote, "You've been
criticizing yourself for years and it hasn't worked. Try approving
of yourself and see what happens."

Ultimately the takeaway with this exercise is to embrace and
love yourself for who you truly are. While it might be a cliché, it's
true that you can't love others or fully receive love from others
until you love yourself.

EXERCISE 6: INTO THE LOOKING GLASS

HERE'S AN OFFSHOOT OF THE previous exercise: Stand no farther than two feet from a mirror and simply gaze into your eyes for five minutes every morning and every night—no affirmations and no judgments. Just look into your own eyes with neutrality. Have you ever done that in your life? How often do we simply gaze at our own image without assessing or judging ourselves? I'd venture to say never.

This exercise is about staying present with yourself. It's not easy—five minutes will seem like an eternity. Slowly but surely, however, if you practice this with regularity, you'll start to ease into a more impartial sense of being present with yourself.

- STICK WITH IT: Yes, it might feel weird to gaze at yourself. But think about it: How often do you look deeply into your own eyes? What do you see?
- BE PATIENT: Five minutes will seem like an eternity. You might even feel like a stranger to yourself. Keep going.
- THANK YOURSELF: You've come this far in life, with whatever trials and tribulations have come your way. Try to quietly express gratitude for the experience of being present with yourself.

EXERCISE 7: SELFLESSNESS BOOT CAMP

WHEN I WAS A KID, I loved being at the house of one of my best friends, Theresa. It was a beehive of purposeful activity: her father was a doctor who worked in Africa (Doctors Without Borders type of work), and each summer he brought home two refugees to live with his family for a year so they could have an American experience. And so there were always interesting people from various parts of Africa plus their large family and friends at their dinner table, exchanging ideas and sharing insights. The house felt like a mini version of the Peace Corps, exciting and fascinating to me. I learned so much being steeped in African culture. I grew up in San Diego in an area that was mostly all white. Not much variety in culture. So I loved the Africans' clothes, accents, artistic abilities, everything.

> **The point is to get out of your comfort zone and experience the deep satisfaction of helping others. By stepping outside yourself to help others, you're actually able to see yourself with more distance.**

Years later, I experienced that same energy volunteering at an orphanage in war-torn Iraq, where I'd gone on a soul-seeking quest to explore my father's homeland. I was filled with a sense of purpose and even exhilaration: if I touched just one life, or changed one child's perception of their future, I was immensely fulfilled. I momentarily stepped out of my own head and into a bigger, more meaningful sense of self.

And so I offer this exercise knowing firsthand the emotional rewards of putting yourself aside in service of others.

Here's how this exercise goes:

- FOR ONE WHOLE MONTH, SPEND two to three hours each week volunteering or doing some kind of charity work. If you're already passionate about a cause, you'll know where to look. If you need a place to start, check out VolunteerMatch.org or Idealist.org for lists of nonprofit and charitable organizations in your area.

- NOW HERE'S THE KICKER: DON'T tell anyone about your activities. Not a peep! Why? Because this isn't about getting accolades from others. It's about practicing not-so-random acts of kindness for the sheer value of giving selflessly.

- DEDICATE YOURSELF TO THIS SERVICE. Journal about it. Ask yourself: What was my volunteer experience like? What did it feel like *not* to tell people about my service? What did you learn about yourself during the experience?

If you've never volunteered like this, you'll probably experience a level of discomfort and resistance. You'll come up with all sorts of excuses. (*I don't have the time!* will be No. 1 on that list.) And the outcome of your volunteering efforts might remain unknown, but that doesn't matter. The point is to get out of your comfort zone and experience the deep satisfaction of helping others. By stepping outside yourself to help others, you're actually able to see yourself with more distance. And that helps you gain a meaningful perspective on your own life.

EXERCISE 8: THE SHAME GAME

SHAME IS THE "MOST POWERFUL, master emotion," author and researcher Brené Brown claims. We all have it to various degrees. It's partly "fear that we're not good enough," writes Brown. "Because true belonging only happens when we present our authentic, imperfect selves to the world, our sense of belonging can never be greater than our level of self-acceptance" (*Daring Greatly*, 2013). But it's also more than that: Shame is generational. It's cultural. It's ingrained in our society through deep-seated prejudice and ignorance. If you're marginalized by long-standing social injustice, "true belonging" is even more complicated and shame runs deep.

According to Brown, shame needs three ingredients to grow: secrecy, silence, and judgment. If you douse shame with empathy, however, it slowly gets extinguished. And two ways to do that is to own your shame and to practice self-forgiveness—that is, to practice empathy toward *yourself*.

Our Imposters have figured out all sorts of ways to circumvent or suppress shame, and thus they prevent us from being in touch with our Authentic Selves. We blame others. Or we stuff shame deep into our psyches, where it metastasizes into self-loathing. Or our shame might accumulate around different circumstances: Maybe we lied to someone we loved. Or cheated on them. Maybe we were unnecessarily harsh with a loved one, causing them emotional pain. Or we drank away our sorrows and became an alcoholic, eventually eroding our friendships, family life, and partnerships.

Owning our shame, not ignoring or dismissing it, is the first step toward emotional freedom. Forgiving ourselves for that shame is the second step. Here's a simple way to start that process:

- WRITE AN HONEST LIST OF all the things you feel shame about. Don't censor yourself. They might be shameful things you did to someone else, or that someone inflicted on you. Get them out on paper. Be specific: What exactly happened? What words were exchanged? When? Where were you? How did you feel?

> **Owning our shame, not ignoring or dismissing it, is the first step toward emotional freedom. Forgiving ourselves for that shame is the second step.**

- HOW DID THESE EXPERIENCES SHAPE your beliefs about yourself and the world at large?
- READ THE LIST OVER. ALLOW yourself to experience whatever emotion comes up, but remind yourself that the experience does not define you.
- WRITE A LETTER TO EACH person who was involved in the shame you experienced, even if you were the person who did something "shameful." Let that person know how you felt. Again, don't censor yourself.
- REVISIT THE "INVENTORY OF HURTS" exercise. Say to whoever was involved with the shame, "I hereby return this shame to you. I release it back to the world and to the past."
- PRACTICE SELF-FORGIVENESS: WE ARE ONLY human. We are all flawed and imperfect. We all slip up and

do or experience shameful things. Give yourself permission to let go of your shame. Remember that it does not define you. If you can't get to higher ground with yourself, consider working with a life coach or therapist to drill down deeper into your shame so you can move through it.

- BURN YOUR LIST IN THE same way you burned the list in our "Inventory of Hurts" exercise.

EXERCISE 9: YOUR VISIONARY MISSION

THESE DAYS THERE'S A LOT of talk about the Big Why. Author and motivational speaker Simon Sinek has made a career of it. In his first book, *Start with Why* (2009), Sinek encourages leaders and entrepreneurs to focus not on what they do, but on why they do it. "People don't buy what you do," he says. "They buy why you do it." In other words, people are motivated by purpose. For example, Apple Inc. has been so massively successful not because it focused on its computers (the "what"); rather, it focused on the *why* behind them: giving people the freedom to be wildly creative.

The Big Why is all about understanding your purpose: What's of value to you? Where do you find true meaning? What do you want to put out to the world? Companies write mission statements to get clear on these questions so they can position themselves in the highly competitive business market. But individuals like yourself can write personal mission statements—or what I call your "Visionary Mission." Once you're clear on your purpose, the Universe has a way of aligning things in your life that are in tune with it.

> **The Big Why is all about understanding your purpose: What's of value to you? Where do you find true meaning? What do you want to put out to the world?**

Here's another way of looking at it: Finding purpose in life is like identifying your North Star. In precise terms, a North Star holds still in the sky because it's closely aligned with the North Pole. Look at it from any place on Earth, and it will be in the same spot, faithfully indicating where due north is. Literally speaking, keeping your eye on the North Star focuses you in the right direction. Metaphorically speaking, knowing where and what your North Star is helps you *consistently* align your actions with your values. It helps you focus in the right (emotional, personal, professional) direction. Having a Visionary Mission statement for your life is like having your own North Star.

Your Visionary Mission statement doesn't need to be complex. In fact, the simpler, the better. Ask yourself the following questions:

- What is meaningful to me?
- Where do I find value in life?
- Who are the five people I see most (you are an amalgamation of these people)?
- What kind of life legacy do I want to have?
- What experiences do I want to have in life?
- What do I want to create or manifest in the world?
- Who do I envision myself to be in one year?

Then write up a one- or two-line mission statement. For example, let's take a look at people who are well known in the media:

Oprah Winfrey: *To be a teacher. And to be known for inspiring my students to be more than they thought they could be.*[6]

---

6. Jessica Stillman, "Here Are the Personal Mission Statements of Musk, Branson, and Oprah (Plus 7 Questions to Write Your Own)," *Inc.*, May 29, 2018, https://www.inc.com/jessica-stillman/how-to-write-your-own -personal-mission-statement-7-questions.html.

Maya Angelou: *My mission in life is not merely to survive, but to thrive; and to do so with some passion, some compassion, some humor, and some style.*[7]

Amanda Steinberg: *To use my gifts of intelligence, charisma, and serial optimism to cultivate the self-worth and net worth of women around the world.*[8]

Will Smith: *Improve lives. The concept of improving lives runs through the center of everything I do.*[9]

One way to keep your Visionary Mission statement alive is to create a vision board. It's a visual reminder of your values and the experiences you want to manifest in life. It's a time-tested exercise that just about everyone loves:

- CUT OUT MAGAZINE IMAGES AND words that represent your dream life and ideal legacy. Fill this board with images of people you admire and aspire to be, the style or sense of fashion you would like to have, the career and types of relationships you hope to attain, the countries you want to visit or live in, and the jobs you covet.
- DISPLAY THINGS ACCORDING TO BABY steps and phases. You can't magically set your mind to

7. Maya Angelou, "My mission in life is not merely to survive, but to thrive; and to do so with some passion, some compassion, some humor, and some style," Facebook, July 4, 2011, https://www.facebook.com/MayaAngelou /posts/10150251846629796.
8. Amanda Steinberg, "To use my gifts of intelligence, charisma, and serial optimism to cultivate the self-worth and net-worth of women around the world," Swipefile.com, https://swipefile.com/amanda-steinberg-mission -statement/.
9. MotivationHub, "Will Smith's Life Advice Will Change You: One of the Greatest Speeches Ever," May 30, 2018, https://www.youtube.com /watch?v=jUzxY3rgbkI.

climbing Mount Everest and just "get there" by visualizing it. You have to take countless steps, prepare, and practice. There are stages and cycles to the process of getting to the top of anything. So lay out your images to correspond to these stages.

For example, if you're an aspiring actor, think about the milestones you need to achieve: Acting school. Auditions. Getting an agent. Memorizing scripts. Cultivating your network. Find images that correspond to these steps and get them on your vision board.

- IMAGINE YOUR WORLD DIVIDED INTO several parts and organize your board according to Mind, Body, Heart, and Soul.

  Mind: What are your daily thoughts and affirmations? What are you reading?

  Body: How do you want to feel physically? What makes you feel good? What feels like *you*? What baby steps can you take to make your body stronger and cleaner? (It can be as simple as walking, getting more sleep, and drinking more water every day. Remember: our bodies are like plants—in addition to food they need air, sun, and water to grow.)

  Heart: Who do I love and who loves me? How open is my heart?

  Soul: What sorts of activities feed your soul— travel, books, spirituality, a prayer, art?

Remember that using images like this is not about being someone else; it's about drawing inspiration from the world around you and having a visual reminder of the mission statement that you want to guide your life.

EXERCISE 10: RETURN TO WONDER

HERE'S A BEAUTIFUL QUOTE FROM poet Walt Whitman that sets the tone for this exercise: "After you have exhausted what there is in business, politics, conviviality, love, and so on—have found that none of these finally satisfy, or permanently wear—what remains? Nature remains; to bring out from their torpid recesses, the affinities of a man or woman with the open air, the trees, fields, the changes of seasons—the sun by day and the stars of heaven by night."

Whitman is one of countless poets and philosophers—never mind ordinary lovers of the outdoors—who understood the deep healing power of nature. The power of nature is not to be underestimated, literally: Studies have shown that hugging a tree increases levels of the hormone oxytocin. This hormone is responsible for feeling calm and emotionally centered. When you hug a tree, you are upping your happiness hormones. (Yes, let's all be tree huggers!)

Personally I've had experiences with nature that are transcendent, even mystical. I was in Nepal years ago, wandering through vibrant golden temples filled with holy men and snake charmers, enthralled by the powerful energy of Kathmandu. But in the Himalayas, in the midst of stunning tree-studded foothills, I had a close encounter of the miraculous kind with a rock. That's right, a *rock*. It's hard to describe the moment without sounding like I'd smoked several pounds of *something*. (I assure you that was not the case.) I was walking down a rocky path with the whole world spread out around me. A profound stillness was in the air. Suddenly, as I continued down the path, a rock drew me toward it. It called out to me. I can't explain this rationally, but the rock said: "Return to ignorance" and "connect with yourself." I pondered the words. *Why would I want to return to ignorance?*

How much more connected to myself could I get? Was I talking to myself? I almost laughed at myself, thinking, *Lisa. You are listening to a rock. Hellooo? Are you nuts?* Jokingly, I said goodbye to the rock. As I turned to walk away, it answered, "Live without a future in mind." I stopped again in my tracks, looked back at the rock, then smiled and strolled peacefully away.

Months later I understood what the rock meant: Forget about everything you've been conditioned to think and feel about yourself and the world—all the harsh parental judgments about the world. Reboot your life.

Being present in nature is a way of returning to wonder, and returning to wonder is a salve for the soul. It's as simple and as profound as that. Simply being present in nature is a form of meditation in action. Experiencing beauty in the everyday world distances you from your impetuous Imposters, and you begin to see yourself with necessary distance.

- TAKE A MOMENT TO STEP outside in nature. Gaze at anything: a flower, a dancing spot of sunshine between the leaves or on the sidewalk, the clouds moving in the sky.
- TAKE A DEEP BREATH AND return to some of the hurts you were able to process in the earlier exercises. If they are not fully released, visualize these hurts. Imagine them in your mind's eye packed inside a cloud that drifts away in the sky and eventually vanishes. Say goodbye to them. Let them go in nature.

EXERCISE 11: CLAIM YOUR MORNING

IN HER RENOWNED BOOK *The Artist's Way* (1992), author Julia Cameron describes the daily practice of doing "morning pages," which is stream-of-consciousness writing you do for twenty minutes every morning before you start your day. The pages "clarify our yearnings," she writes. "They keep an eye on our goals. They may provoke us, coax us, comfort us, even cajole us, as well as prioritize and synchronize the day at hand. If we are drifting, the pages will point that out. They will point the way True North. Each morning, as we face the page, we meet ourselves. The pages give us a place to vent and a place to dream. They are intended for no eyes but our own."

Doing morning pages is just one practice that allows you to claim your morning and set intentions for the day. But you can do *any* contemplative practice: yoga, meditation, taking a walk in nature, stretching, saying a prayer, doing affirmations—or even just having a cup of coffee or tea in stillness. Starting your morning in a contemplative practice, in silence and in relationship with yourself, sets a positive foundation for the rest of the day. (The alternative? Start your day rushing, and literally pump stress into your body, which sets the foundation for the rest of the day.)

Starting your morning in a contemplative practice, in silence and in relationship with yourself, sets a positive foundation for the rest of the day.

Author and life coach Tim Ferriss describes the importance of morning rituals in his book *Tools of Titans* (2016). Ferriss has five morning rituals that include meditation, exercise, making his bed, morning pages, and drinking special tea. He's happy when he consistently does three of them, but the point is that he has them. "If I hit three out of five, I consider myself having won the morning," he writes. "If you win the morning, you win the day."

Here are the five simple things Ferriss suggests we do every morning:

- Make your bed.
- Meditate.
- Do five to ten reps of something.
- Prepare "titanium tea."
- Do your morning pages.

MANIFESTING CHANGE AND SEEDING THE soil for personal growth takes practice and commitment. Like with any form of exercise, you need to commit and do it regularly. We all know that small things done strategically over time yield big results.

In the case of the preceding exercises, if you incorporate even a few of them into your life on a regular basis, you'll see change. You'll experience transformation, have aha moments, feel a keener sense of purpose, and prepare the ground for personal insights. And, of course, you'll also be more acutely aware of your Imposters and how they trip you up.

The only way to begin is to begin. And the only thing getting in the way is you. It sounds so simple, doesn't it? Well, what are you waiting for?

SOME FINAL WORDS

Congratulations, dear reader! You've made it through your SoulBlazing journey! I'm thrilled that you're now ready to apply the principles of this book in your own life. From this point forward, you should understand how your own dominant Imposters play out in your life *and* in other people's lives.

The great thing about this process is that it's simple yet profound: There are seven key archetypes or masks that we wear. We start wearing them at a really young age, and we let them define us (or hinder us) for most of our lives. But once we understand these seven key Imposters, we start to look at life through a different lens.

The Imposter framework helps you quickly cut through your own negative self-talk and push yourself out of your comfort zone. It also helps you clearly see and understand *other* people's discomfort zones so that you don't go down relationship rabbit holes. You start to have insights into how people hurt each other. You even have aha moments about how *you* might hurt other people or undermine your own best interests. Given free rein, the Imposters sabotage all sorts of opportunities for growth and keep us stuck. They reinforce patterns that don't serve us, and

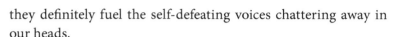

they definitely fuel the self-defeating voices chattering away in our heads.

But when you learn how to understand the seven Imposters and harness their superpowers, you make meaningful change in your life. You start to cultivate a sense of purpose and passion, and you ultimately get in touch with your Authentic Self and your Authentic Soul.

This process isn't always easy, but let's face it: few things worthwhile in life are, and nobody's perfect. We're all human, which means that we're all flawed. There's no such thing as perfection. In fact, the Japanese concept of *wabi-sabi* suggests that there is beauty in all things imperfect and impermanent, which I believe is true. So bear in mind that understanding your Imposters is not a way to become a perfect human being or even to strive for perfection. It's about cultivating self-awareness, purpose, and authenticity so that you maximize the equity in your life. By *equity*, I'm referring to the value and meaning in your life, rather that something with a price tag. As I described in the exercise "Write Your Own Eulogy," equity is about measuring your life against the values that feed your Authentic Soul.

Having an ongoing S.O.U.L. practice will help you cultivate the life in your years as described above. If you do this practice on a regular basis—if you *STOP, OBSERVE, UNDERSTAND, and LIBERATE* yourself from negative beliefs and thoughts—I promise that you'll experience growth. And that growth will give you the insights you need to overcome obstacles in life. Because here's another news flash for you: Obstacles and suffering are inevitable. They're part of the human condition.

Viktor Frankl, one of my superheroes, was a neurologist, psychiatrist, and Holocaust survivor. Frankl knew all about suffering and the human condition. His harrowing experience in concentration camps and his extraordinary will to live are the subject of his life-changing book *Man's Search for Meaning*

(1946). Writes Frankl: "When we are no longer able to change a situation, we are challenged to change ourselves."

The earlier tools and exercises are designed to help you put into action all the principles in this book. They're designed to help you explore how your Imposters play out in your life. I've written about the value of getting out of our comfort zones in earlier pages, and I'll reframe it again here: We all have various degrees of comfort addiction. In fact, we have more comfort addiction than at any other time in human history because we've never had so much comfort at our fingertips—literally! (Just think about it: we take so many things for granted that were unthinkable just a few generations ago, from plumbing and electricity to one-click ordering and delivery by drone.) But stay in your comfort zone, and you'll never change, excel, or push yourself to reach your dreams. Your Imposters will keep you in the same patterns, cultivating the same negative self-talk.

On the other hand, if you understand your Imposters and harness their superpowers, you'll be able to manifest purposeful change.

We can all convert hardship into positive growth by utilizing the superpowers of our Imposters, even if that is uncomfortable. Getting out of our comfort addiction is essential. Without it, we stay in the same old no-growth safe zone. We don't change. Life stays on pause. We have to embrace life outside the comfort zone. Remember: The pearl in an oyster starts off as a little particle that builds up its iridescent, gemlike self through constant irritation. Diamonds are formed by constant pressure. Nature is full of examples of this metaphor, which also holds true for us human beings.

Not that personal transformation has to be hard, but the old expression "no pain, no gain" has been around for a reason: We learn through trial and error. Our so-called failures can be our greatest lessons. They are catalysts for growth. And as we grow, we actually cycle through different Imposters. When I was a teenager, for example, my Judge Imposter was on overdrive as I blamed my parents for holding me back by being so protective and not allowing me to take risks. My Victim Imposter eventually pulled my strings, and I blamed lots of people for holding me back. As a young adult in Hollywood and Japan, my Seductor Imposter took center stage to survive in a competitive industry, only to be unseated by my Fixer Imposter when I went to Iraq to explore my roots, to try to fix myself and others I loved, and to eventually become a life coach and educator.

Let's never forget that we all have free agency and free will. Each one of us has a choice: We can find reasons to stay stuck. We can blame other people or circumstances at large. We can let fear guide our lives. We have a choice of how to respond to each situation as we morph through different Imposters while going through challenging times, just like in the five stages of grief: we're first in denial, then anger, then bargaining, then depression, and finally acceptance. When we get to a point where we can love and forgive ourselves and others, we will be reborn and will be able to respond to life instead of reacting. Then we can get moving and blaze our own souls. Everything in this book is dedicated to that goal. In other words, it's all about SoulBlazing, which is the ultimate gift you can give yourself.

ACKNOWLEDGMENTS

No book gets written by just one person. I believe it takes a village to bring forth great knowledge into the universe. My name is on the cover, but everyone I mention here and many others (you know who you are) have contributed to the collective of what I call *SoulBlazing*, including the father of archetypes, Carl Gustav Jung.

I'd like to thank my family, starting off with Lee Aronsohn, for being in my corner from the beginning of this journey and believing in me. He was instrumental in helping me get my first book published, *Whispers from Children's Hearts*. I'm also grateful that our relationship helped create and hone the Imposter Model. Thank you to Ava for making me a mom, cracking my heart open, being a bright light in my life, and helping me evolve.

Thanks to my parents for giving me life and teaching me about cultural diversity and love at its deepest levels. Your encouragement and strength helped me through many hard times.

And to my sisters: Julie, Lila, Alix, and Sandy, with whom I've shared many wonderful and life-changing journeys. We've laughed, cried, loved, and grown together.

I'd like to give gratitude to my creative Soul Family for supporting me and bringing magic and inspiration to my life for decades after I moved away from home in my early twenties to chase my dreams: Fred Powers, you have been my rock and teacher for over thirty years. David Bergeaud, for opening me up to my spiritual journey of voracious traveling and reading. Randall McCormick, for being a loving and masterful teacher when I started my writing journey. Bill Meyers, for allowing me a front-row seat to the magic of Hollywood, which inspired me to reach heights I thought I could only imagine, and to the legendary Ben Vereen, a lifelong dear friend and confidant. To my besties, who have been my heart for the past twenty-to-thirty years. I've loved growing up together and holding each other's hands on this creative, epic journey called life: Eve Selis, Theresa Moujaes, Deborah Kagan, Glenda Shaw, Gayana Ravelle, Maria Conchita Alonso, Lynn Rose, Wendy Zahler, Luis Colina, Kyle Wilson, Ray Shaolian, KC Wisdom, Ric Gibbs, and Paul Patti.

In addition, Anoop Kumar, Dr. Gurmeet S. Narang, and Bobby Joyner, whom I've never met in person but who have deeply contributed to my life in such a meaningful way through our Zoom or phone conversations, reminding me how our souls are interconnected.

To my master coach, Steve Hardison, for providing spiritual surgery and helping me connect with my higher self. He truly possesses a gift of communication that changes lives.

To all my clients and the brave SoulBlazers out there who have passed through fear, grief, and other life challenges by using the Imposter technique and having their souls blazed.

To my publishing company, Girl Friday Productions, for being so detail-oriented and showing such commitment to this whole process.

A special thank-you to Frank Ferrante, who read the earlier draft of this book and encouraged me to get this out. His sensitivity and brilliance helped me articulate my stories.

My niece, Daniella, for always being supportive and reading several drafts of my books throughout the years and giving great notes.

A special thank-you to David Marsh, for being such a supportive friend. Your contributions with producing and shooting content for *SoulBlazing with Lisa Haisha* have been invaluable.

Finally, I have a debt of gratitude to my editor Debra Ollivier. Debra's keen editorial expertise, creative insights, and stellar ability to connect vision to prose helped bring this book to light. We had great working mojo and became dear and trusted friends along the way.

Many thanks to my friend and creative genius Daniel Will-Harris. He created my website, logo, and Imposter icons, and he inspired this book cover. He was terrific to work with and will continue to be part of my creative team.

ABOUT THE AUTHOR

Photo © Ragan Photo

LISA HAISHA IS A LIFE coach, author, transformational speaker, TV host, and avid traveler. She holds a master's in spiritual psychology. Her fascination with people has taken her to over sixty countries, where she has worked in everything from boardrooms to yurts, helping people make shift happen in their lives. She is also the chairwoman of Silicon Valley's Pitch Global LA chapter, and she frequently works with entrepreneurs to help them manifest change.

In addition to offering private coaching and retreats, she has interviewed and filmed dozens of movers and shakers and out-of-the-box thinkers to explore what makes them tick. The *Legacy Series* led to the Amazon Original *SoulBlazing with Lisa*

Haisha and inspired two more documentaries: *SoulBlaze Your Life: Conversations with Master Teachers* and *Encounters with Metaphysical Healers.*

For more information, visit these platforms:

Soulblazing.com. Learn about the coaching and retreats Lisa offers.

Whispersfromchildrenshearts.org. Check out Lisa's humanitarian work and discover how you can participate in the movement.

YouTube: youtube.com/c/LisaHaisha. Find out more about Lisa's adventures and teachings.

Facebook: facebook.com/lisa.haisha

Twitter: twitter.com/LisaHaisha

Instagram: instagram.com/lisahaisha

LinkedIn: linkedin.com/in/lisahaisha

CPSIA information can be obtained
at www.ICGtesting.com
Printed in the USA
FSHW022115260122
87952FS